Vagabonding Through Retirement

Unusual Wanders Far From

Our Paris Houseboat

by

Bill Mahoney and Ina Garrison Mahoney

Copyright © 2015 Bill Mahoney and Ina Garrison Mahoney
All rights reserved.

ISBN: 1500985856
ISBN 13: 9781500985851
Library of Congress Control Number: 2014920060
Create Space Independent Publishing Platform,
North Charleston, South Carolina

Thanks to our friends and family for their help and encouragement.

Contents

1 *Wanderer* · 1
2 En Route · 7
3 A Mooring Hurdle · 13
4 The Interlude · 19
5 *Le Bienveillant,* Our New Home · · · · · · · · · · · · · · · · 22
6 The Fixing Up · 26
7 On the Trail of… · 32
8 Morocco: Kif · 38
9 Morocco: On to the Kasbah · · · · · · · · · · · · · · · · · · 44
10 China: We Wend Our Way · · · · · · · · · · · · · · · · · · 48
11 China: Down the Yangtze on The East Is Red · · · · · · · · · · · 56
12 China: Not Even a Smattering · · · · · · · · · · · · · · · · 61
13 USSR: To Moscow on the Trans-Siberian Express · · · · · · · · 66
14 Thailand: Keeping Your Cool Is the Golden Rule · · · · · · · · 71
15 Thailand: Down the River on a Bamboo Raft · · · · · · · · · · 78
16 The US of A · 84
17 Thailand: More Jingle Bell Encores · · · · · · · · · · · · · · 91
18 Thailand: Sea Gypsies · 97
19 Laos: Up the Mekong · 101
20 Laos: Two Dinners and a Blessing · · · · · · · · · · · · · 108
21 Bali: Beach · 115
22 Cambodia: Smoking the Cobra · · · · · · · · · · · · · · · 121
23 Cambodia: Living on the Edge · · · · · · · · · · · · · · · 126
24 Bali: Land of the Monsoons · · · · · · · · · · · · · · · · · 132
25 Bali: A Transformed Kuta Beach · · · · · · · · · · · · · · 136

26 France: A River, a Taste of Mustard, and Wine · · · · · · · · · · 140
27 Bali: Good-bye, 1900s · 145
28 Romania: Gypsy and Dracula Country · · · · · · · · · · · · · · · · 149
29 Romania: Constanta · 155
30 Ukraine: Not Too Far to Chernobyl · · · · · · · · · · · · · · · · · · 158
31 Ukraine: On to Odessa · 164
32 Vietnam: Ho Chi Minh City · 167
33 Vietnam: "Not Saigon Again!" · 175
34 Morocco: Couscous and Camels · 183
35 Turkey: "But You Said No Monuments!" · · · · · · · · · · · · · · · 192
36 Peru: We "Blaze" an Inca Trail · 201
37 Peru: Machu Picchu · 207
38 Bolivia: Our Hotel near the Witches' Market · · · · · · · · · · · 213
39 Bolivia: La Paz's Most Bizarre Prison · · · · · · · · · · · · · · · · · 219
40 South America on His Own · 223
41 United States and Australia: Home Exchanges · · · · · · · · · · 229
Epilogue · 235

1

WANDERER

(Bill)

I BOUNDED UP the steps of the Amsterdam public library two at a time, oblivious to the cold March wind whipping up my collar. A lifelong drive for adventure prompted me to quit my humanities teaching job in Belgium and come here to search the "boats for sale" sections of the Dutch newspapers. My new career plan: buy boats, take them to Paris, and sell them for a handsome profit.

First I needed a boat to live on. Most listed were more than I wanted to pay, but one in Friesland looked promising, so I drove my VW camper to Leeuwarden and found the canal where she was moored.

The minute I saw her, I was smitten. She was an old, sixty-five-foot leeboard sailboat with a round bow—they don't make those anymore. She no longer used her sails, so she'd been outfitted with a motor. The emblem of a Lister, a good motor, was affixed to her black smokestack, and a red banner with a yellow dragon waved from the top of the tall oak mast. She was painted green, and the teardrop-shaped wings that raised or lowered on the leeboard side to stabilize her in strong winds were painted green and white. Even her name—*Zwerver,* meaning "wanderer"—was appealing. Ever since I was a kid, I'd been a wanderer, and when Ina retired from her job at Supreme Headquarters Allied Powers Europe (SHAPE) in Belgium we planned to continue wandering the world.

That afternoon I tested the foghorn and revved the motor. The neighbors must have realized the *Wanderer* had a new owner.

I called Ina the minute I thought she'd be home from school.

"Got exactly what I came for!"

"Already? That was fast!"

"Yeah, I got lucky. And she's a beauty. Can't wait for you to see her."

Next stop for the *Wanderer* was a shipyard. I knew the granite rule: take a boat out of the water and check the hull before you buy. Since I hadn't, I realized how lucky I was when Herr Draaisma, the yard's owner, said, "You need a couple of plates replaced. Otherwise she's in good condition."

Since the work wouldn't take long, I asked if he knew a captain who could take me to Belgium.

"I know the perfect man, but he doesn't speak much English, only Dutch and Frisian."

That couldn't have been better. Languages are my hobby. Since Frisian is the closest to English, I would enjoy hearing it spoken. "Can he take me as far as Ghent?" I asked.

"No, his wife is sick. He's retired, but won't leave her for more than a day. But that's time enough to get you across the Waddenzee."

"The Waddenzee! Everyone says that route is much too dangerous. The boatman all advise me to go by canal."

"Then you haven't been talking to real sailors," he said. "It's dangerous for them, but this man keeps his own boat there. He knows that sea as well as the letters in his name."

The day after the repairs were complete, Captain de Gref arrived ready to go. With his blue cap, big hands, and nimble movements, he appeared capable of commanding anything. To celebrate his return to the wheel he brought a bottle of gin. Before we got underway, I joined him for a toast.

It was a bit foggy when we arrived at the old stone lock in Harlingen, the entrance to the Waddenzee. Perhaps more than other ports, the windswept facades of the buildings along the canals and the weathered faces of the sailors spoke to me of salt and sea.

My captain's enthusiasm had increased—he gave four extra toots, along with several exultant waves, when his friends opened the lock. After we got out in the open sea, he asked if I'd like to take over and get a feel for my boat. "I'll sit over here in the wheelhouse and keep you on course," he said.

I reveled in being at the wheel, feeling I was doing what I was meant to do, taking to the open sea, steering my own boat. Retirement was even better than I'd dreamed.

My enthusiasm dampened when the wind started blowing and the water became rough and choppy. At the sight of two red flags, I turned to ask my captain to take over, but he had moved to the corner of the wheelhouse and was leaning into its angle, sucking on his gin bottle.

I pointed to the red flags and shouted above the wind, "Where do I go?"

He blinked several times. Raising a hand, he muttered, "*Rechtvoord.*" Blinking some more, he waved in another direction and muttered another "*Rechtvoord.*"

I hadn't a clue which of his "straight aheads" was valid. "Where do I go?" I shouted again above the still-rising wind.

He rose for a look but lost his balance; his now-empty bottle rolled across the deck. There was no time to help him up; I had to make a decision. I chose to go through the two red flags. There was a scraping sound, and we stopped.

I shook his shoulder and shouted, "What do I do now?" I grabbed my bottle of water and doused his face. "We're grounded! What do I do?"

He sputtered a bit as he made a few more useless hand flutters.

I knew these leeboards were flat bottomed, so I put her in reverse and gave her full throttle. Ever so slowly, she eased off the bank.

I wasn't sure which direction I should take, but after studying the warning flags, I took a wide course around the one on the right. Ten minutes later more red flags appeared. Again I shouted at my skipper. This time I got a mumbled, "*Rech.*"

There was nothing to do but go ahead and hope. Neither worked. In fewer than fifty yards, I was stuck on a second sandbar. This time when I reversed full throttle, nothing happened. I turned the wheel to the right. No movement. A hard left. Still nothing.

The wind was now smacking one side of the boat so hard I thought it might knock us over. The sun was nearing the horizon, so it would be dark before long. Scenarios raced through my head. I felt sure I could save myself, but what about the captain? Was my retirement dream about to go under? And what about Ina?

I was working one of the life preservers over the captain's head when I saw something on the horizon. A mirage or a real ship? Not waiting to find out, I raced down the stairs, grabbed a yellow blanket, climbed to the roof of the wheelhouse, and waved.

It was a ship, and it was coming my way.

After he assessed the situation, I heard the captain say "coast guard." He pointed to his watch, raised his open hand twice, and gave me a thumbs-up.

It probably wasn't more than ten minutes, but it seemed like an hour before the cutter approached. It was almost dark by the time a sailor threw me a line, and the cutter began towing me off the sandbar.

In total darkness my *Wanderer* coasted to a naval base at Den Helder and came to rest twenty meters from a submarine. A stone-faced lieutenant came aboard and demanded my papers.

"Didn't you know a storm was coming tonight that would have ripped a hole in your hull?" he shouted.

"No, sir, I didn't," I answered. I explained about hiring Captain de Gref and the gin.

"Eugene de Gref?" The lieutenant's manner changed. "Why, we go to the same church. He knows the sea better than I do."

De Gref must have heard his name and realized who was shaking his shoulder, but the lieutenant still had to guide him along the rail and onto his boat. I knew he wouldn't want to face me in the morning, so I left an envelope for him. I shouldn't have given him a cent, but in retrospect this adventure was worth the money.

Peter, Herr Draaisma's choice to take me from Den Helder to Ghent, arrived the next day. He was a burly redhead, about thirty-two, and so skillful you would have thought he'd been born on a boat. I later learned he had been.

Despite the sandbar incident, the *Wanderer*'s steering system and rudder worked fine, and the Lister motor purred, steady and reassuring, while we motored south.

"How did you end up in Holland, Bill?" Peter asked.

"Well, I've always liked boats. I sailed with the merchant marines and then spent three years in the Pacific on a navy carrier."

"I thought Herr Draaisma said you were a teacher."

"I was, but I got into teaching through the back door."

"The back door? What does that mean?"

"It means while I was in the navy, I went to night school. A year after my discharge, I graduated from an adult high school in Seattle, Washington. Then, thanks to Uncle Sam, the GI Bill gave me a second chance. It paid my way through UCLA."

Peter let me take the wheel so he could show me how to hang out while we waited to enter a lock. For him it was nothing. He knew when to throttle and when to coast. It wasn't so easy for me.

"Why did you buy this boat?" he asked.

"I guess because I'm a wanderer. At fourteen I heard the open roads call. While other kids were going to high school, I was roving the States."

"What did you live on?"

"I'd pick up odd jobs: packing celery in Florida, running errands for gamblers in the French Market in New Orleans, fitting pipes in a shipyard in California. After I got my degree, I landed a teaching job for the US Army in Paris."

Near the town of Zaandam, north of Amsterdam, Peter turned into the Noordzeekanaal. As we headed south, in the direction of Delft, he asked why I would leave Paris to teach in Belgium.

"It wasn't by choice. De Gaulle kicked the NATO forces out in '66. I was transferred to SHAPE."

"What was it like being there with all those generals?"

"Because of those generals, our facilities were excellent. The students came from fourteen different nations. But after teaching for twenty-three years, I was ready to move on."

Before we entered the powerful current of the Scheldt River, Peter arranged for a hookup. For a few guilders, a thousand-tonner tugged us through those hazardous currents. Four days later we arrived in Ghent.

After Peter and I shook hands and said our farewells, I called Ina and told her to come meet me on Friday after school. I was eager to see her and for us to get the *Wanderer* to the French border.

2

En Route

(Ina)

I SHOULD HAVE suspected that Bill underplayed his danger on the Waddenzee. He had done such a great job emphasizing his good luck in finding "the perfect boat" that I wasn't the least apprehensive the next morning about his captaining the *Wanderer*.

After he got us underway, we arrived at a drawbridge stretched across one of Ghent's main intersections. I squeezed the rubber ball on the red-tasseled brass horn that was kept in the wheelhouse. The bridge master smiled down at me before he lowered the barriers to stop traffic. When the bridge parted, Bill motored through, and we were on our way to the French border along a beautiful, tree-lined canal.

Except for holding on to a branch while Bill tied us up on Saturday night, my only duty was to keep my captain watered and fed. The *Wanderer* was Dutch clean on the inside. It had everything Bill needed, including a bedroom and a kitchen with a stove, small fridge and dishes. There were four chairs and a table, and a bathroom with a shower and toilet.

I spent the day in the wheelhouse on a stool beside Bill, peering into the cabins of passing boats. I saw one woman with a basket of clothes walking precariously close to the edge before she stepped up to the arched metal hull covers to hang a blue shirt and some work clothes. It was as though she were in her backyard. Another woman at the wheel zipped by while breastfeeding her baby.

On Sunday morning we moored near other boats at the French border. The *Wanderer* would remain moored there while Bill found a captain to take us to Paris; we would wait for spring break so I could go with them.

A couple of nights before our scheduled departure, while we were eating pizza, Bill mentioned the captain he'd engaged had an accident and couldn't take him. Then over ice cream he said, "I haven't been able to find anyone else who's free."

A delay meant I couldn't go with him. "So what are you going to do?"

"Oh, the two of us won't have any trouble getting her there."

"That can't be legal, can it? In France we'll be on rivers, not just canals!"

"Sure, it's legal. See, I'm authorized," he said, whipping out his license. "I'm required to have a second person along for safety reasons."

I looked at the license, but didn't read the fine print. I remembered well his taking lessons. Thinking of the trip, which I mentally labeled "My Picturesque Canal Journey through the Belgium Countryside," I agreed to go along—for safety reasons.

On the morning of our departure, Bill got us "unparked" and through the French border with no trouble. All went well with my initial assignment; I was to sit at the bow and signal if we got too close to the bank. Before arriving at our first bridge, I made my way back—pardon me, aft—to ask what the signs meant. I pointed toward the large triangles above the arches of a bridge we would be going under.

"They designate which one we should take," Bill said.

"So which one is it?"

"I think it's the yellow one, but I'm not sure. Don't worry. It doesn't matter. Nothing is coming."

That made me uncomfortable, but we were coming to the first of many locks we would have to go through, so I focused instead on his new instruction. "Tell me whether the entry light shows red or green."

I called, "Red," and Bill hung out to wait his turn. Then it became obvious the light was green, not red.

"It's not easy to stay in one place with an underpowered motor," Bill said.

My explanation? "In this fog I wasn't sure, so for safety reasons I thought it prudent to call red."

Once we got inside a lock, I was to throw a rope around a bollard to hold us in place while the water levels adjusted. The hearty riverboat women made everything look easy, so I wanted to emulate them. But I didn't look the part, not wearing my bright-green garden gloves with a white ruffle.

As we switched between canals and rivers and back to canals and again to rivers, entering locks became hectic. I don't remember the sequence or whether they were in canals or rivers since there were locks in both; I just remember the worst of the "awfuls." In one of the multistory locks, where the water levels were so different between the river and the canal, I got the loop over the first bollard, but when the water came rushing in, I delayed too long with the flipping-off part. My line first pulled tight and then got tighter. Bill had to run up to chop through the rope so we could rise to the next level.

In another lock I missed tying us up so our bow began to swing out. The lock workers used their gaffs to keep us from bashing the other boats. They shouted insults. I had no time to look their way, but was thankful I wasn't conversant in some French words.

Soon after we entered the Sambre River, Bill asked me to take over while he took a toilet break.

"Relax," he said. "This is a long, wide stretch, so all you have to do is just keep us going straight."

I was doing that until a doublewide barge loaded with sand came around the bend. "Bill!" I yelled. He didn't answer. "Bill!" I screamed louder. I thought the barge was coming straight at us, so I moved over to give it more space.

Bill heard the scraping and came hurrying up the ladder to cut the motor. He went back down to pull up some floorboards. I joined him, beseeching Neptune to keep us afloat.

When no leaks appeared after several minutes of anxious pacing, Bill gave me a reassuring pat. I felt relieved until he said, "We could have a broken rudder." He continued with his inspection. "Bad news. One of the welds holding the rudder cracked. Since it's the weekend, I probably won't find anyone to repair the damage until Monday."

I should have been dismayed. I wasn't. How wonderful a whole day and a half without duties would be!

Bill's persuasive powers were in high gear. He not only found someone to do the welding, but Sunday morning he waved to a passing barge and got the captain to pull us away from the riverbank.

Bill's skills had improved during the week, and he was even enjoying himself. I, however, spent my days looking forward to mooring. My nights were dream filled, but my worst nightmares were preferable to the *daymares*.

"You can relax now," Bill assured me two days later. "We're coming to the very modern Canal du Nord, so we won't be on a river for a while."

We did fine until we got into the canal's tunnel. Without running lights we could barely see beyond the bow of the *Wanderer*, so Bill eased back to dead slow. When the ship behind us had to slow to keep from hitting us, a hefty woman jumped out of her cabin and ran along the towpath. Shaking her fist, she shouted something I translated as "Move your bloody ass!"

Bill's quarter throttle wasn't enough to appease her. Back in her cabin, she blasted her horn. After the first blast, the boats behind joined in. Their echoes reverberated through the rest of tunnel's darkness.

One evening we couldn't find anywhere to moor until Bill spotted an appropriate tree along the river's bank. But this tree was back from the bank, which would mean I, a nonswimmer who is afraid of water, would have to get off the boat to tie us up. I had no choice. It was getting dark.

Bill maneuvered closer. I gritted my teeth, threw the rope around the bollard, slid off the boat, waded to the bank, and pulled. The boat didn't move. I watched the rope slide off the bollard and fall…into…the…water.

Bill found another rope and tied it to the bollard, threw the end to me and I secured it around the tree. As I climbed back aboard, I wondered if this trip would ever end. It was only 150 miles to Paris by road. I could drive there in less than three hours. How could it take nearly two weeks by water?

Our last fiasco occurred when we tried to get diesel at Conflans-Sainte-Honorine, where the Oise rushes into the Seine, augmenting the already swift current. When Bill tried to pull in, we shot past the station. He didn't remember that a dock must be approached against the current—yet another bit of river lore we didn't possess.

Bill was all for making another attempt. I wasn't.

"OK," he said. "If we run out of fuel, I can pump some from the heating tank. It's the same stuff, only a different color. Using it is illegal because governments subsidize it."

"Could you possibly think that our breaking another French law would concern me?"

The next day, while passing though the last lock, the gates began to close when we were only three-fourths through, but we got out safely and motored up the Seine into Paris. We passed the French replica of our Statue of Liberty; I might not be a huddled mass, but I *was* yearning to breathe free.

Bill reached a spot not five hundred yards from the Eiffel Tower and tied up between two signs I knew had something to do with illegal mooring. But my nautical career had ended! I didn't wait for him to do the honors; I popped the champagne cork.

On my two-hour train return to Belgium on Sunday, I did some serious thinking about Bill's new career. It was still OK with me if he wanted to buy boats and bring them down from the Netherlands to France, but never again would I be talked into being his co-captain. And when I retired, I'd know to buckle my seat belt. Any trip with Bill was sure to be bumpy.

3

A Mooring Hurdle

(Bill)

I FELT GREAT. My beloved *Wanderer* and I were in the heart of Paris. When I got back from going to the train station with Ina, I went to sniff around the other houseboats for information.

A middle-aged fellow sitting on the deck of *Simpatico* saw me. "Hello. Did you bring her down from Holland?" he called out.

"Yeah, got her in Leeuwarden."

"Come aboard and have a coffee."

Bob was a former American navy pilot. He poured me a cup and passed me a croissant. "Where do you intend to moor her?" he asked.

"Somewhere in the center."

"Good luck, but I'm afraid you don't have a chance. The waiting list is long. You need pull, and even then it's hard."

"How'd you get here?"

"Six years ago it was easier, and my girlfriend's mother has connections. They keep the waiting list secret and shuffle the privileged to the top."

"Hardly fair."

"Not much in politics is."

"What does that parking sign mean?" I asked, pointing to the one where I had moored.

"Twenty-four-hour limit."

"Do they enforce it?"

"You'll have a knock on your door tomorrow."

"What will they do if I ignore them?"

"They'll get you out. I've never seen them tow anyone away, but the longest anyone resisted was a German guy who lasted four days."

"How'd they get rid of him?"

"Sealed up his boat. They only let him back on board to leave. See the yellow-and-green boat across the river?"

"Yeah."

"Owners' name is de Lessep, the family of the engineer who planned the Suez Canal. Takes clout to get a place these days."

It was eight thirty the next morning when I heard a bang on my cabin door. An official, blue-paneled truck was parked outside with the door open—the driver must have figured his business wouldn't take long.

"Don't be here tomorrow," he said. "Twenty-four-hour limit."

"But I have to be in Paris for my research."

"Twenty-four-hour limit. No places in my sector."

He went his way, and I went back to my coffee.

On day two he knocked more forcefully. To impress me the flunky flashed his official red-white-and-blue card.

"I have to be in Paris for my research," I repeated.

"No place in my sector."

"I invested in this boat. I can't moor it in my pocket. I have to be in Paris."

"Your problem. Go south to the Marne. There are places there."

"It's too far."

"If you're here tomorrow, you'll be in trouble," he yelled. He slammed the door of my cabin so hard I thought the window would break. He revved his motor and sped off. The bastard was probably headed for a peaceful parking spot to sip on his red wine for the rest of the day.

That night I told Bob what the official had said about the Marne. He laughed. "Yeah, it's right on the southern edge of Paris, and it's the farthest spot from the center. He doesn't give a shit as long as you're out of his area. If you hold tight, he might suggest Boulogne. It's downriver. Sometimes you can get in there, but it's a dump and there's rats."

When the official came the next day, he did mention Boulogne, but I told him, "I am a college professor, and I have no intention of moving into that rat-infested slum."

His face turned red, and his hands clenched as if he were fighting an urge to grab me by the throat.

I stood, calmly shaking my head.

"That's it!" He stormed off, slamming the door, clearly not accustomed to having his officialdom challenged.

I saw him take out a black notebook, so I figured this was the final act. That afternoon I took the metro to Boulogne. The only open spaces were rocky and too hazardous for mooring.

When I got back that evening, a yellow document from the Centre de Navigation de la Seine was on my door. It was a *procès-verbal* telling me to appear before Madame d'Acier at ten o'clock the next morning. The note included the threat of a heavy fine and a list of nasty consequences that would result if I failed to appear.

I went to see Bob.

"Do you know the translation for the name Madame d'Acier?" he asked.

"Yeah, Steel Lady."

"Believe me, she lives up to her name. She has steely blue eyes, and when you enter her office she'll be sitting ramrod straight."

"You mean I should go?"

"You better. That's an official summons. Get ready to leave, Bill. You don't stand a chance."

In the morning I put on my best slacks, a worsted blue suit coat, Italian loafers, and a tie for the first time since I'd left the classroom.

Hoping to be as phony and hypocritical as my adversary, I took my black briefcase with a guide to the Louvre and a French translation of Will Durant's *L'Age de Louis XIV*.

I arrived early on purpose. The secretary glanced at my summons and told me, "You're thirty minutes early." I gave her my sweetest smile and nodded in agreement—she could tell time. She motioned toward some chairs. I chose the one facing the inner sanctum and whipped open my copy of *Louis XIV*.

The secretary opened the door to inform Madame that today's victim had arrived early. The Steel Lady, caught off guard, was leaning back in her chair, smoking a cigarette and reading a book about the Sumerians. Hallelujah! I recognized the cover; I had used it in my classes. I have a special interest in the Sumerians—the people who more than five thousand years ago moved into the land that is now Iraq. Maybe, just maybe, Madame might not hide the book in a drawer when she summoned me. If she did, I would still use my—I couldn't help noticing—approach.

The secretary didn't say another word until precisely ten o'clock. With my French translation of Durant's book in my left hand—the title clearly visible—and my black leather briefcase in the other, I walked in as though I were the dean of Harvard Law School.

My hopes soared when I saw the Sumerian book closed but visible on the desktop. The Steel Lady had my official paper in her hand and a stern expression on her face.

"Why, madame, I see you are reading one of my favorite books. I know every page. I've used it for years with my classes."

"You're a professor?"

"*Oui*, madame."

"Where?"

"UCLA, madame. I have just begun a year of sabbatical leave and have chosen to be here to use your wonderful museums. Anywhere else I could only read about Mesopotamia and Prince Gudea, but here I can go to the Louvre and see his statue."

"How did you come to be on this boat?"

"I bought it in Holland but brought it here since no city possesses the rich culture of Paris. I've been dreaming of this opportunity for ten years."

"But you should have thought of a mooring for your boat. There is no decent place available."

"I would accept any mooring near your libraries and museums, madame, for that is where I will spend most of my time."

"There is only one space possible, and I don't think you would be able to stand the noise or the fumes. It is only ten meters from a main road. Cars stream by day and night."

"Madame, when I am lost in a book, I could be sitting in the middle of a factory and still concentrate."

Madame d'Acier had the secretary bring coffee. We discussed the *Epic of Gilgamesh*. In the next two hours, between cookies and coffee, we climbed a Sumerian ziggurat so high I had her regretting she didn't have a better mooring to offer me.

I told Bob about our meeting.

"You're a real con man," he said. "You actually told her you're a professor?"

"Of course. If she can shuffle the waiting list, I can shuffle the shit."

"Do you realize that triples the value of your boat?"

"Yeah, I figured it did."

He slapped me on the back. "You hit the jackpot!"

"I was lucky," I said, though I knew my new career plans might be shot. Without a mooring, boats would be hard to sell.

"Not just luck. You'll be a legend on the river for piercing her armor."

As I went down the gangway, I said, "Please don't pass the word around. You'll screw me up."

"Don't worry," he called after me. "I edit my stories."

The next day the panel truck pulled up. The knock was civil, as was the greeting, "Oh, I saw your tennis balls on deck, professor. Do you play?"

"Yes, I do." Actually, I squeeze tennis balls when I practice yoga breathing.

My messenger told me he would drive over to the right bank and park on the road leading down to the quay where I could moor. He helped me tie her up. When he said good-bye, he shook my hand, as though I really were the dean of Harvard Law School.

4

THE INTERLUDE

(Bill)

THE ACUTE MOORING shortage had me rethinking my new career plan. While considering my options, I began going to Centre Pompidou where I met people who were there to listen to their free language recordings. I began exchanging English lessons for them teaching me their language.

To help with my lessons, I constructed two books. I had no idea of the number pages they contain since that kept changing as I added cutouts, but I used the books enough to know what was where. I covered the larger book—which I use for comparing similarities in various languages—with black leather from an old jacket. My smaller book contains widely used verbs in first-person present, past, and future tenses in the major languages. By using them, I can make simple sentences and communicate with much of the world.

One day at Pompidou I read an article in *Time* magazine concerning a little-known Irish law granting citizenship to descendants of immigrants forced to immigrate during their potato famines. I fit the bill. Dual citizenship could be advantageous, and I knew learning about my ancestors should prove interesting, so during Ina's spring break we took off to sniff into my roots.

The librarian in Cork was knowledgeable. "Oh my, yes. One of the Mahoneys wrote a well-known song about the bells of our cathedral. But if you're looking for information for a passport, you'll need to go to Dublin."

While I was talking with her Ina discovered a poster about a thirty-second O'Mahoney gathering. On the poster, a lion was standing upright near a fortress wall. The hand attached to an arm was holding a feather above the lion's head. I preened. "Look at that plume. It's just as I expected. I am of literary nobility. Didn't know you were traveling with royalty, did you?"

"Of course I did. If I remember correctly, it was pigs your grandparents owned, wasn't it?"

"Pigs nothing! Let's go to the castle where I will introduce you to my noble cousins."

"Lead on, Mahoney! With so many of you around, I'm sure it will be nothing less than scintillating."

The brochure we received at Dunmanus Castle stated it was erected around 1430 and is regarded as the finest of the eight surviving O'Mahoney castles. It was no Versailles, but I wouldn't admit it was just a rather unimpressive stone tower—Ina's assessment. One lady from Auckland informed all within earshot, "My ancestor, Baron O'Mahony, resided in this very castle!"

The ledgers in the Dublin's archives were larger than telephone books. In the 1869 volume, I found—John Mahoney, son of James Mahoney. John had married a Nora O'Hare, but the name I had for my grandmother was Nora O'Hern.

The genealogy specialist studied it. "The name is blurred," he said. "Why don't you try to get the baptismal certificate from Cork?"

I called, and Father O'Reilly found the O'Hern record. Armed with this and a statutory declaration, Ina and I headed back to Paris to file my papers.

On the way she began reading *The Birth Certificate Issued in Pursuance of Births and Deaths Registration Acts 1863 to 1872*. It was a foot long and almost as wide. "So that feather on the Mahoney coat of arms stands for literary nobility, does it? Did you happen to look at column eight for the signature of one of the witnesses? It has Molly O'Hern, her mark an X. Now, let me see…Molly must have been…your grandmother's sister."

"Well, I notice you didn't check on your Fitzgerald ancestors."

"I didn't need to check on the Fitzgeralds. Everyone, but everyone, knows about their connection with John Fitzgerald of the Kennedy clan."

I didn't have time to reply before she started laughing. "Column five—'dwelling place of father: Backwater Course.' That is a classy address. And have you read 'rank or profession of father' in column seven?"

"So he was a laborer. That's a hell of a lot more honorable than bootlegging whiskey like your Fitzgerald-Kennedy connection."

After this trip Ina said, "If we're going to be traveling around Europe, I'd rather have more comfort than the VW offers."

Had the dollar not been at its highest ever against the French franc, we would have settled for something less than a Mercedes James Cook model.

As I now had a place to live with both a shower and a toilet, I sold the *Wanderer*, and I made more than Bob's predicted "three times its worth with a mooring."

I still owned *Le Bienveillant*, a houseboat on the outskirts of Paris in Port Marly. Since it didn't have a motor, and Ina knew I wouldn't be moving it, she agreed to live there.

I was ready for us to move into my nearly hundred year old houseboat when June came and Ina retired.

5

Le Bienveillant, Our New Home

(Ina)

I was excited when Bill drove us to our new home. I knew her name, *Le Bienveillant,* had several connotations—kind, caring, benevolent—all with a sense of warmth I hoped I'd feel if we ever got aboard. But it was noon, and there was no sign the young musicians who had been renting it were leaving.

It's hard to be unaware of movement on a gangway, so we walked down under the keyhole-shaped archway the boys constructed with thick vines they collected from the island across the river.

Pedro, a drummer from Brazil, came out. "Bill, could you give us a couple more weeks? We haven't found anywhere to put all our equipment."

"Sorry, but I've scheduled a trip to the boatyard for tomorrow."

An hour later Pedro reappeared. "We're ready to leave, but we'd like you to join us for a farewell toast."

Six of us sat at the table in the glassed-in entrance room with its 180-degree view. Though it desperately needed a coat or two of paint, I felt sure this would become the favorite spot. From where

I was sitting I could look out at the thick-growth island across the river and upstream there was a colorful lineup of many shaped houseboats.

Their neighbor, Michel Ange, opened a bottle of wine to toast the boys' pleasant stay here. The boys then proposed the next toast to our future life aboard. I so wanted to excuse myself for a look around, but willed myself to stay put.

It seemed hours before final handshakes. As Bill helped them carry their equipment up the gangway, I began my inspection.

After descending the two steps into the hallway, I went into the kitchen. I'd been sneaking peaks at it through the three-foot square opening between the rooms. I liked the idea of being able to stay in a small area to prepare food in a galley kitchen and then passing it through the opening so we could eat in the entrance room. But before I did any cooking, I'd need lots of Lysol to sanitize everything.

Next to the kitchen was a small bedroom. There a pulled down bunk, reminiscent of a real ship, caught my eye.

Bill joined me in the living room at the end of the hallway. "That fist-sized hole in the wall by the telephone happened when George found his girlfriend was cheating on him," he said. "You have to admit the paint job in here is as colorful as they are."

"Yes, I'm sure these passionate-purple walls would have shown up well under their strobe lights."

"I've always like that oval oak table," Bill said, nodding toward the dining alcove. "I bought it the same year I bought this boat. It opens up and will seat ten."

On the riverside a second hallway had an extra long closet with sliding doors. "Great!" I said. "That's big enough to hold all our clothes."

I then saw our small bathroom. "We'll have plenty of work in there."

In the large bedroom, crumpled cigarette packs littered the floor, and a stained mattress rested near the sagging bookcase that was attached to the wall.

Bill then opened the door to the furnace room. I had a long look before saying, "When that hand-pumped toilet and the urinal are moved out, then we'll have room for our freezer. Everything will work out—eventually."

After this tour, I realized my dream of settling in when our furniture was shipped from Belgium was just that: a dream. We'd need to accept Michel Ange's offer of help with fixing her up. But on that long-awaited first night, we settled in the pull-down bed in the small bedroom. The moon shone brightly through the window. We were content. We were home—two retirees on the Seine in the outskirts of Paris, on *Le Bienveillant*, our kind and benevolent houseboat.

The next morning when I returned from the *boulangerie*, I saw Bill's feet sticking out of the opening of the storage area that was under the entrance room.

"What in the world are you doing down there?" I asked.

"Saving the boat," he answered.

"Saving the boat!"

"There's six inches of water here. But don't worry. We won't sink. We'll be on our way to the boatyard in a few hours."

By noon the tug to take us hadn't arrived. Bill called repeatedly—no answer. He spent the night trying to slow the leak. I didn't sleep either. The next day a boat arrived—the type that pushes barges loaded with automobiles.

As it pulled up beside us, Bill said, "That much power will damage our boat."

"Don't worry," the captain assured him. "I know what I'm doing."

We did worry, but getting to the yard was urgent. It didn't allow time for discussion.

We arrived in record time and when they glided our boat up the ramp, water cascaded from the hole. After the pressure hoses sluiced off forty or more years' worth of accumulated muck, the foreman's hammer taps revealed more problems. He explained the work needed and repairs got underway.

Bill took the precaution of renting an empty barge to protect our mooring place—claim jumping does happen. He wrote letters informing the mayor and the navigation authorities we would be at the shipyard for at least a week. When we returned he wasn't surprised to find a letter from the mayor.

> Cher Monsieur:
> I wish to inform you we are installing more pontoons at the rowing club to accommodate the additional boats we acquired after the construction of our new building. They will cover part of the space you occupy; therefore you are required to leave your mooring immediately, or I shall take the necessary steps to have you towed away. There are no other places available in Port Marly.
> Permit me, my dear sir, to send you my most sincere and distinguished greetings.
> Monsieur Le Marie

"Damn, damn, damn! He means it. He'll tow us away," Bill said. "What are our options?"

"We don't have any unless we find another mooring. The mayors who use the rowing club have the power. They'll tow us. I've been checking regularly and there aren't any moorings. But come on, we have to do some rechecking. It's our only hope."

6

THE FIXING UP

(Ina)

When we returned from our fruitless search, Bill pulled into the lane in front of the rowing club. M. Roussis, a twinkly-eyed riverboat man who had grown up diving for sponges off the island of Rhodes waved for us to stop. He had shown Bill the treasures he had discovered during his thirty years dredging the Seine. Bill was especially fond of the bronze sword from the period when Vercingétorix battled Julius Caesar for control of Gaul.

"Heard about your problem, Bill. I've been waiting to catch you to tell you I've retired. My wife and I are moving to Normandy. None of my boys want to live here, so you can have my mooring."

Overjoyed, we both hugged him.

"Bill, except for floods is there anything more that can happen to us?" I asked as we walked in.

"No, but all houseboat owners have to be gamblers."

While Bill installed us far enough from the rowing club for their new pontoons, I cleaned and waited until he got hooked up to electricity, water, and the telephone before I asked, "Do we have enough power for our dishwasher, microwave, washer, dryer, stove, and deep freeze?"

"Afraid not."

The father-and-son team Bill chose to rewire the boat balked at removing the masses of antiquated 12-, 110-, and 220-volt wires. From experience we knew France is never accused of being consumer friendly. It was only after Bill removed the old wires they would begin the rewiring.

I also wanted the old water-storage tank we didn't need replaced with kitchen cabinets.

"There shouldn't be any water in it," Bill said. "It hasn't been used in years."

As a kid I'd acquired thumping experience testing watermelons to see if they were ripe. I thumped the tank. "Sounds empty to me." I said.

Bill's mechanical ability may be zero, but he's skillful at demolition. He screwed a pulley into the ceiling, attached ropes around the tank, and anchored them on the heavy iron kitchen radiator.

"Move into the hallway just in case," he cautioned.

I moved, and Bill disconnected the fifty-gallon tank. Fortunately he was standing by its side when the pulley snapped and the tank came crashing down. Bill was laughing so hard I couldn't understand his first comment—something about watermelons. "Why didn't I drill a hole in the damn thing?"

I agreed, and added the sink board and the kitchen floor to my growing list of needed repairs.

We made frequent trips to the other side of the island to Communauté Emmaüs, an organization similar to the Salvation Army to buy used tools and supplies. When I saw Bill buy a queen-sized sheet, I assumed it concerned a language project. I knew I was right when I saw him on his hands and knees with his black Magic Marker writing:

Cultural Exchange
Échange Culturel
Free English Lessons
Leçons d'Anglais Gratuites

I teach English in exchange for any other language.
J'enseigne l'anglais en échange pour tout autre langues.

I had questioned his calling it a "cultural" rather than a "language" exchange. "Few of the characters you meet exhibit a high degree of taste and refinement."

"I'm using the connotation 'the totality of socially transmitted behavioral patterns.'"

"Oh!"

It was bad enough sitting in places where he displays his small sign. How was I going to ignore a queen-sized sheet? In fairness, I'll admit that over the years Bill had introduced me to some "interesting characters."

The bathroom came next. Bill called plumbers. Houseboats and plumbing aren't compatible. No one wanted the work. He finally found Tony, an Italian, who agreed to take a look, but he couldn't come until he finished two other projects.

With the bathroom on hold, Bill loaded the camper with books, including Shakespeare in Spanish, French, German, and Italian.

This is the story he told me when he returned—without the camper: "As usual there were cars with emergency lights flashing, waiting for arrivals to stream out of the metro. I waited and watched. At the right moment, I swooped into the occasionally used area nearest the curb and hurriedly stacked Spanish, French, German, and Italian books on the dashboard. I jumped out to attach my sheet.

"By the time I was seated in the back with the sliding door open, five people were reading my sheet. An elderly lady speaking impeccable French said, 'What a wonderful idea! Do you speak any Khmer?'

"Only a few words. I find the pronunciation difficult.

"'Then I can help you with that. But I'm afraid one of the letters in your greeting is missing.'

"Oh, then I copied it wrong. Would you fix it, please?

"While she was correcting my mistake, two police officers stopped.

"When I took the arm of my charming, eighty-year-old first client to help her step up into our van, I noticed the metro manager watching. After she sat in the jump seat facing me, I opened my book and read: *Niak ch'muah çi?* She smiled at my pronunciation of: What is your name?

"One of the police officers nodded his approval, and the metro manager, who was ready to pounce, saw her too, so he didn't make me leave. This lady saved me.

"The day went so well I left the camper in place and took the metro home."

Bill assured me it would be safe. I hoped he was right.

While Bill spent his time at the metro stop, I was being creative—my *Reader's Digest Handyman's Guide* wasn't full of workable solutions for old houseboats. It took only two coats of textured white paint to obliterate the boys' purple walls and hide my wall-patching job.

When Tony arrived to look at our bathroom Bill spoke to him in Italian. "We need a new washbasin and toilet here."

"This room is too small."

"I think it will work," Bill continued in the same calm manner, "if the toilet replaces this bidet."

"What kind of bathroom will you have without a bidet?"

Bill explained this facility was not part of the usual American bathroom so we could do without it. "We'd like a tiled shower here," indicating our small shelf bathtub—the type seen in western movies where the cowboy tucks his knees under his chin for his Saturday-night bath.

"Impossible! You can't have a window in the middle of the shower on the bank side!"

For this Michel Ange supplied the answer. "I can fill in the window and then cover it with a stationary shutter when I redo the outside."

We thought this was a great idea and Tony agreed to take the job.

By this time both Bill and I were ready for a break and I had several suggestions ready.

"Ina, we need to go somewhere you can learn to swim. Have you forgotten your fear when you were co-captaining? If you fall overboard, you need to be able to save yourself."

I hadn't forgotten, and he decided the Dalmatian Coast would be the place for me to learn, so we left Michel Ange in charge and took off in the camper.

At the lake in our campground in Zadar, I put on a life vest to keep me afloat, but I insisted that Bill keep his hands under me until I tested it for reliability. Bill then demonstrated the movements I should make. A few days later, I felt the need to proceed at my own pace. Trying my utmost to sound confident, I said, "You go on and do your thing. See, I have the hang of it now." This was a bald-faced lie, but by keeping one foot on the bottom I could hop through the water and make it look convincing.

When Bill goes to any new place he wants to learn some of their language. One of his techniques is to write a story—a woeful tale of a pretty girl sitting in a park. She is alone with no mother, father, sister, brother, cousins, or friends; and she has no money. She is also hungry, tired, ill, sad, and homeless. In his story Bill invites her to come with him to his grandmother's house, where kind Granny takes care of her. Using his homemade books he translates as much of his masterful epic as possible before he persuades several native speakers to correct and record his story. The two twelve-year-old boys who were helping him couldn't stop laughing. Bill couldn't get his mouth into position to pronounce Serbo-Croatian consonant-loaded words like *krv* (blood).

My swimming subterfuge worked until the day we stopped at a fishing port on the Adriatic. The bottom made an unexpected drop. Finding myself in water over my head, I panicked and began flailing my arms and kicking. Whatever I did worked. I was swimming.

With both our missions accomplished, we returned home.

Tony had done a good job on the bathroom, and Michel Ange had finished installing new shutters and painting the outside, so he and I took turns with the rented sander, and Bill returned to his metro parking spot.

Bill had a dozen regular students from among the many foreign nationals living across the street at the Cité International Universitaire de Paris. Word of his program reached William LeMercier, director of the TV program *France Matin*, the equivalent of *Good Morning America*. Louis, the crew director, along with two camera operators and a sound technician, came to our refurbished *Le Bienveillant* to film the boat and Bill's library. Louis selected ten of Bill's students to exchange a few phrases and then had a linguistic specialist comment about his program.

The metro manager, sporting his bronze nametag, was filmed boasting, "I arranged for Monsieur Bill to park here because I recognized the value of his lessons."

The original title of the program was "The Smallest English-language School in Paris," but it aired worldwide as "A Unique Way of Learning Languages with the Barter System."

7

ON THE TRAIL OF...

(Bill)

ONE DAY WHILE eating falafels at a favorite restaurant on rue Rosier, the heart of the Jewish quarter in Paris, I was in the middle of explaining my newest language project when Ina interrupted to ask, "Are you positive there is such a thing?"

I wasn't, so I skipped that to answer the question I assumed she'd ask next. "With a Yiddish New Testament I can work on three languages at once since the Yiddish and Hebrew alphabets are virtually identical."

"Okay, that's two . . . what's the third?"

"Well, Yiddish is primarily bastard German. I know enough German to begin reading Yiddish which would help me learn Hebrew."

"...Oh."

Ina equates the approach I use with my Bible collection to a third grader attacking Joyce's "Ulysses." I read a phrase such as: "The light of the body is the eye..." in the languages I understand. Then I make a windmill attack on the same phrase in a difficult language. If I'm able to distinguish the word *light* from *eye* I consider my time well spent. Ina doesn't. She frequently asks, "Why do you insist on playing Don Quixote?"

My standard response, "Why not?"

I then read her a clipping from a popular French daily. According to it, the most famous polyglot was Cardinal Mezzofanti (1774-1849) who spoke twenty-eight languages. "Powell Alexandra Jurulus, a Canadian, could translate forty-one." I should have stopped before I got to: "Today it is thought impossible to speak more than ten to twenty-five..."

Ina interrupted me. "And you want to add a twentieth Bible to your collection?" She's convinced I suffer from *dementia linguistica*. So while I searched for a Yiddish New Testament in the bookstores, she went to buy pastrami.

My quest became international at Christmas when we went to Montreal to visit her niece. At the first opportunity I took Ina to the Hassidic quarter. While we walked through it I tried to read the Hebrew letters on the window of the kosher butcher shop. I recognized Yiddish echoes from the delicatessen, so we stopped to look at their lox cream cheese platter and blintzes in the window. I began asking anyone who looked like a rabbi, virtually everyone, about a New Testament. Ina went in to watch bagels being shaped then dropped into boiling water. "If you're going to spend your time chasing a phantom, I'll stay to see them come out of the oven."

I continued but my questions elicited the same puzzled look and negative answers as those I received in Paris.

After a Greyhound Bus deposited us in Atlantic City, Ina suggested I might as well inquire about the Bible at the crap table in the Casino. "You'll be as likely to find one there as anywhere else."

I didn't hit the Yiddish New Testament jackpot, but I did win enough for a couple of great dinners.

Our next stop was at a friend's Chelsea apartment in New York City. One afternoon we helped serve meals to indigents at her Episcopal Church. On other days we visited the Natural History and Metropolitan museums, and many evenings we attended a play or musical. When I read a notice about the Dead Sea Scroll exhibit at the public library we went there to consult their specialist. He searched through his numerous Yiddish references but finally said, "I wouldn't know where to send you. None are currently in print."

In the spring, still focused on finding my Bible, we complied with all the regulations imposed by their communist governments, and took off in our camper van for Eastern Europe. We exchanged the mandated amount of money, and registered with the police in Prague as required. Prague, like Rome, was built on seven hills, but rather than looking for a campground, I parked on a level, quiet, tree-lined street in the heart of town. Ina was reading from the guidebook: "Prague's architectural marvels rise in splendid harmony on both banks of the Vitava..." My door opened and an arm pulled me out of the van while a soldier shouted, "Documents!" The guards looked over our passports, tossed them both toward Ina, and ordered me back inside. As if I were a mosquito, he flicked his hand for us to leave.

"So much for *splendid harmony*," Ina said. "You parked in front of the Soviet newspaper *Pravda*."

While she admired the *architectural marvels* I drove around until I located a place along the riverbank to spend the night.

In the morning, Ina, though reluctant, accompanied me up one of the hills to the Strahov Library which houses one of the largest Bible collections in the world. I felt confident this was where I could dispel her skepticism. She hung back while I spoke to the librarian.

I left after a brief exchange.

"It's going to be rather difficult to find what doesn't exist, isn't it?" Ina said.

Nonplused, I strolled across the Charles Bridge, past its *thirty historic statues* toward the ninth century Jewish ghetto. Before all of Hitler's massacres there were around a hundred thousand Jews in Prague. Today there are twenty thousand. I wanted to inquire at the Jewish Zidovske Museum so I approached the four men dressed in black who sat at the entrance counter. All had beards and were at least eighty. Their wide brimmed hats hung on hooks behind them. I had made the same inquiry several times, but I still felt more than a bit awkward asking, "Have you ever seen a New Testament in Yiddish?" From the way they looked at one another, it was obvious none of the thousands of visitors had ever asked this question.

The man who stamped tickets recovered first. "We had a librarian once who knew most everything ever written in Yiddish. If anyone would know, he would."

"Could you give me his address?"

"I'm afraid he doesn't live here now. He's in Budapest."

"Can you tell me how to find him? We're en route there."

I thanked him for the phone number and we went in to visit their museum. It contains one of the most important collections of Jewish artifacts in the world. Ina strolled around examining the kosher knives and the double chairs used for circumcision while I scanned titles in the library, just in case.

Next I visited their cemetery where I located one grave dating back to 1439. And I was able to decipher the Hebrew letters for *Joseph* and *Simon* on tombstones. Ina wasn't impressed. Instead, she searched for the tomb with the most pebbles placed on top—she said this custom signified love and respect.

The next morning we left for Hungary. On the outskirts of Budapest we looked for a telephone booth, but it wasn't until we got to the center that I found one. When I got through to Mr. Saltzman, he was not only aware a New Testament in Yiddish existed, he knew of a bookstore that had one.

Halleluiah! Not wanting to waste time, I left Ina in the camper and took a taxi to the address he gave me.

The bookstore was in a residential neighborhood. Before I closed the door, I blurted out, "A Mr. Saltzman told me you had a Yiddish New Testament."

"Yes, a most unusual book."

"Could I see it?"

A stack of books interrupted our conversation—a man dropped some as he came through the door. The owner helped pick them up and they began discussing prices. I was so excited I began searching his shelves for my Bible. I hadn't located it so when the man left I hurried back to the counter.

"That was a most unusual book. Never seen another like it. Had it on my shelf over a year. Sold it two weeks ago."

Shit was what I thought; "Oh no," was what I said.

All he could remember was it had been published in Berlin, maybe in the eighteen nineties, but it was a publisher he had never heard of.

With no other leads to follow we returned to Paris with Ina's unhelpful, "Well, at least you now know it exists, but I doubt you'll ever find one."

For more than a year, my search was on hold. One day on my way to Centre Pompidou, I stopped at Kentucky Fried Chicken to use their toilet. Half a dozen young men sitting at tables wore red tee shirts emblazoned with the Star of David, and JUIFS POUR JESUS. I asked the closest one my Bible question but before he could answer the leader interrupted, "Do you believe in the resurrection?"

Ignoring his question I asked, "Have you ever seen a Yiddish New Testament?"

"Yes, I have two of them, but why do you want it?" the leader asked.

On hearing this, I prepared to fall to my knees, swear my firm conviction in the resurrection and add the Virgin Birth. I answered, "To improve my Yiddish and learn some Hebrew."

"Bibles are not for language learning!" He said this with such vehemence I realized any declaration of faith now would prove futile. After several deep breaths I addressed him in the calmest voice I could muster, "If you need both of yours, would you be kind enough to tell me where they were published?"

"Baltimore, Maryland."

I copied the address.

Less than a month later, the bell above the gangway of *Le Bienveillant* clanged and the postman handed me a package. I noted the sender had paid $12.00 postage. A note inside read:

> Dear Mr. Mahoney,
> This Bible is out of print, so we no longer have copies for sale, but we had this one on our shelf that you may have free of charge.

Deeply grateful for the generosity and kindness of the Lewis and Harriet Lederer Jewish Foundation, I waved my treasure at Ina, "You're right!" I crowed. "I didn't find my Yiddish New Testament around any corner, but who the hell would have thought I'd locate it in the Colonel's Chicken Coop?"

8

Morocco: Kif

(Ina)

I sidled up to Bill and said in a sultry voice, "Take me to the kaaas-baaah. I sound like Ingrid Bergman, don't I?"

"Not really."

"Then I'll keep practicing. I want to use this line when we get to Morocco."

Bill's sister and her husband were on a cruise and were docking in Lisbon. We would be there to greet them, but wanted to go to Morocco first.

At the Spanish port of Algeciras we drove our camper onto the ferry to cross the Strait of Gibraltar. When we disembarked on the continent of Africa we learned we were still on Spanish soil—a result of Morocco's checkered history. In the nineteenth century, she had been a protectorate of Spain as well as France.

After we drove around the Spanish military base at Ceuta, we set our watches back to GMT—which for some reason all time zones in Morocco follow. Had we gone by their lunar calendar, we would have lost more than six hundred years, as their year one begins with Muhammad's migration to Medina in what is our 622 AD.

Two men wearing red armbands blocked the road before the entrance to their border. Holding up a roll of money, they announced, "This is where you change money." This ruse often works because it's illegal to import or export *dirhams*. I had been duped on my first trip here, so I told Bill to drive around them. We smiled and waved.

A few yards farther, we pulled into the real border, where a nice-looking young man directed us to a parking place. He stuck his hand through my window and said, "Passports!"

I was holding them, so I handed them over. Bill said, "I don't think that was a wise move, Ina."

It wasn't until the fellow cut to the front of a long line that I realized what he meant.

Bill grabbed the fellow's arm. "Give me back our passports. We'll wait our turn!"

He ignored Bill.

After our passports were stamped, the hustler motioned for two uniformed officials to check our camper.

While checking, one of them discovered the small tear gas spray Bill kept above our bed. With a disdainful look, he said, "Morocco does not permit anything as barbaric as this!" He handed Bill a receipt. "If you show this on your way out, it will be returned."

The hustler walked to the hidden side of our van and held out his hand. Bill handed him a dollar and a couple of packs of American cigarettes—we don't smoke, but they're welcomed as tips. The fellow pushed both away.

"I saved you an hour," he said. "I deserve at least ten dollars!" Ten dollars is more than many Moroccans earn in a week.

Bill took back the cigarettes and dollar and strolled over to the money-changing window. The hustler followed and pushed his shoulder against Bill. Bill took his time placing the dirhams in his billfold before walking back to the camper. He got in and started the motor. The fellow moved in front of our van and raised his arms. Bill revved the motor and moved forward just fast enough to oblige the man to get out of the way.

"Our muscle man is in cahoots with the police," Bill said as he drove away. "They might try to get revenge."

Thoughts of reprisal kept flashing through my mind, so I watched for a police car to pull us over. Our van would be easy to describe—it's white, and because of its shape we referred to it as "the pregnant hippo."

Bill had come to Morocco seeking beach time, so I read out the choices from my guidebook, and he choose Oued Lao, described as "a young tourists' gathering place." It was about fifty miles away—not as far as I would have liked.

Just before we arrived, he found a likely looking spot, zipped himself into his wet suit, and carrying his speargun headed for a group of rocks at the foot of a cliff. I checked the van's doors and curled up in the back to read what our book had to say about the area.

A few minutes after Bill left, a knock sounded on the window by my head, and a voice called, "Open!" in French.

I jerked back from the window and answered with a defiant, "*Non*!" I wasn't about to open the door for anyone.

The man walked around and pounded on the side door. Then he moved to the front. "Open!" he shouted, trying the handle of the door. Finding it locked, he went to pull on the back door. Although my pulse raced, I felt sure it would be safer to ignore him, though I knew he slapped his hand flat against the side window to hold something close enough for me to read. After more futile window slapping, along with what I assumed was Arabic cursing, he stalked off.

He was back quite soon with Bill in tow. I opened the side door and Bill got his passport and handed it to the fellow, who was wearing what I realized was a uniform. He checked each page of Bill's passport. He then asked for mine.

"She's the most stubborn woman I've ever seen," he said.

He allowed Bill to stay and fish but he kept our passports. "You can pick them up at the police station when you leave."

"Police Station! Bill, I don't want to go near one!"

"It would be better if you were more careful next time," Bill suggested.

"Me? Be more careful? What do you mean?"

"Well, after all, I'm driving, so I can't be expected to do everything!"

This was his usual line when we pulled a dumb stunt, but I did wonder how both of us had missed seeing the large signs—THIS IS A RESTRICTED MILITARY ZONE.

Bill went back to spend more time in the water. He didn't spear any fish; it's rare that he does, but he insisted he'd missed a huge one by less than an inch.

After picking up our passports and checking into the Oued Lao campground, we went into town and stopped at the first café. Before my mint tea was served, I said, "Bill, the smoke in here is worse than downtown Bangkok at noon."

"The smell of the smoke tells me the beach isn't the major draw in this gathering place," Bill said.

While drinking his beer, he made contact with Mustafa, a Berber in his midtwenties. Berbers, Afro-Asians, had been the early inhabitants of North Africa and still outnumbered the Arabs in rural areas. Mustafa felt sure the military suspected us of being connected with *kif* (hash) because on moonless nights, speedboats made runs carrying it from this area to Spain. "The police often arrest tourists at the border because smugglers tape drugs underneath the frames of their cars. If they aren't arrested, the smugglers follow them to remove it after they cross into Spain."

Mustafa explained that none of the restaurants in town would open until the universities' terms were over in two weeks. "If you stay until then, you'll see this town come alive."

To me that meant more smoke. I already needed to breathe some fresh air, so we strolled along the beach, looking for some kind of food. We walked the entire length of the town, but all we found were sardines being grilled in a makeshift barrel. They were good, but a complete meal of sardines wasn't the gourmet meal we had looked forward to having in Morocco.

On our return to the campground, I noticed ours was still the only vehicle. My earlier unease about police reprisal had not abated, so before going to bed, I checked to make sure we had locked all four doors. As for Bill, he was sleeping within two minutes. We had made a quick trip down through Barcelona. Our only long stop had been at the Alhambra in Granada, the Moorish palace that's straight out of the *Arabian Nights*. I lay awake for a long time, listening for approaching footsteps, but all was quiet…almost too quiet.

After a few hours an awful sound woke me. I bolted up.

"What's the matter?" Bill mumbled.

"Someone's being murdered," I said. The sound came again, louder and closer.

"Sounds like a donkey to me," he said and turned over.

I peeked out of the curtain and spotted a little brown burro placidly chewing grass not more than ten yards from us. I felt foolish, but relieved enough to get back to sleep.

The next day Bill proposed we go to the nearby town of Souk al Sabt. He knew *Al-sabt* meant "Saturday," and Moroccan towns were often named for the day of their *souk*, or market. With no restaurants open, we needed food. Besides, we never resist the temptation of a market.

Bill asked Mustafa if he wanted to join us, and on the way we picked up two elderly ladies. Bill doesn't enjoy the bargaining process, and I have no skills. But watching our women passengers, who were bent on not spending a *centime* more than a date or a tomato was worth, was high drama. That evening I opted to stay in the van to eat our produce rather than inhale kif smoke and dine on sardines again. Bill went alone to meet Mustafa and came back with the news that the Moroccan government still tacitly allowed Berbers to grow cannabis in the Rif Mountains—they had helped one of the Moroccan kings fight both France and Spain for independence.

I wanted to see it growing, so the next morning Bill drove us up a steep, winding road leading away from the beach. The kif looked lush in the fields, and acres and acres of it grew among the zigzags and hairpin turns. When we returned, two motorcycle cops were negotiating with the driver of a truck, so they waved us on. "Mustafa told me these cops demand payoffs from the truckers who sell the kif elsewhere," Bill said.

We spent the rest of the day biking. Two young girls deserted their herd of goats to block our path.

"Please, let us have a ride!" one pleaded with Bill in Arabic. Her friend took my bike. The aggressive one tilted Bill's so she could straddle the bar. She first pumped the right pedal and then shifted, so she could reach the left one. She continued shifting while she followed her friend down the dirt road. But after a few hundred yards, she missed a shift and tumbled into a bush. She made it back, flashing a bright smile and ignoring the scratches on her arms and legs, unaware that the back tire was deflating. In her excitement she thanked Bill in both Arabic and French: "*Shoukran beaucoup.*" Her form of "thank you very much" is now one of our favorite expressions and was worth having to walk back to town because of a flat tire.

9

Morocco: On to the Kasbah

(Ina)

As we left Oued Lao the next morning, Bill stopped to ask a young fellow walking up a steep hill if he would like a ride. The fellow couldn't believe his luck. Holding on to the door while he looked our camper over, he said, "This will be my very first time in a car!"

I moved to the back so he could sit up front and have the whole experience. He examined everything on the dashboard and turned numerous times to study every facility in the back. We learned he would spend five days at school, memorizing the Koran, before making the long walk back to his village. When we stopped to let him out, he was too shy to kiss our hands and thank us a half-dozen times, as many Moroccans do. Instead, after he got out, he held on to the door until he could present Bill with an egg from his food sack. Bill hesitated for fear he wouldn't have enough to eat that week, but knew he had to accept it.

On the outskirts of Fez a hustler on a motorcycle pulled up to Bill's window with an offer to guide us. Bill engaged him, as this city that was founded in the 9th century is an unbelievable maze.

From a previous visit, I learned that getting to the tiled western gate to enter the souks is difficult. And once inside, the markets are a tangle of passages difficult to navigate, but Bill was looking forward to the challenge, confident his few words in Arabic were good enough to get us around.

On our arrival twelve or more potential guides, ranging in age from ten to fifty, surrounded us before we got out of our van. As much as they wanted their one-dollar fee, they hoped we would buy a rug, jewelry, or something so they would receive a commission.

Bill tried an Arabic phrase. It had no effect. He pulled loose from their clutching hands. "Ina, let's have a mint tea."

Who came to stand around our table? Who shouted the entire time we drank our tea? Admitting defeat Bill pointed to one of the five who insisted he was a struggling student. After his selection it was if he had clapped his hands at a flock of crows. The others disappeared in search of another prospect.

Shouts from the men unloading produce from the backs of their donkeys greeted us when we walked through the gate. Milou, our chosen guide, shepherded us through a couple of antique stores and made sure we had ample time to inspect their beautiful carpets.

We stopped to look at the water clock invented during the Middle Ages to inform people when it was time for their prayers. The clock was no longer functioning, but it was easy to see when one of the twelve troughs filled with water, an hour had passed.

Bill wanted to see the oldest university in the world so we stopped by their Madrassa Karueein, founded in 859 AD.

Before joining the large group watching the leather dyers, Bill bought us sprigs of mint. We held it to our nose, though nothing could mask the gut-wrenching stench of the fifty or more wet skins spread out in the sun to dry.

Men whose legs were the same red, black, blue, or yellow as the dye stood in circular vats. When a skin bobbled to the top they used their long poles to push it back under the surface. It was a fascinating scene and we stayed as long as we could stand the odor.

Our guide was worth the two extra dollars we gave him. Bill was still confident his Arabic would have gotten us around. I didn't believe that any more than I understood why leather dyeing was considered a prized job to be handed down for generations.

The afternoon we arrived in Tangier, Bill drove down by the dock. He had first visited this city the year before it became part of Morocco—when it was a wide-open, international territory and a haven for exiles, expats, and questionable commerce.

"I'm just going to take a quick look to see how much it's changed," he promised.

I wasn't thrilled being left alone in this strange port as night was setting in, but Bill assured me I'd be OK. I locked my door and moved to the back to watch the street activity from behind the curtains. Only minutes after he left, Bill's door opened, and a head wearing a black wool hat peered in. My heart pounded, but my arm shot out with adrenaline force. Leaning over the seat I gave the head a shove. I yanked the door shut and made certain it was locked before double-checking all the other doors and windows.

It was more than "just a few minutes" before Bill returned. I didn't have time to blurt out what had happened before he said in a matter-of-fact tone, "The fellow who scared you is the security guard. He asked me to tell you he's sorry he frightened you, but he didn't know you were in the back. His job is to verify all cars are locked."

It took a few deep breaths to return to calm, but the lemon chicken with olives at the restaurant across the street was delicious. By the time we finished our meal, I was agreeable to spending the night parked there on the street rather than roaming around in the dark, searching for a campground that was supposed to be somewhere out there on the edge of the city.

Our guardian knocked on the window when his shift ended at three. After Bill paid him, I went right back to sleep as he assured us Abdul, his replacement, would look after us.

The next day Bill led me through Tangier's narrow streets, pointing out the palaces and the Grand Mosque in the oldest part of the city. "Aren't you pleased I was thoughtful enough to bring you to the kasbah without your having to ask?"

"I do so appreciate your thoughtfulness," I said, realizing he had outfoxed me.

We stopped at the notorious le Café de Paris in la Place de France where many clandestine deals were planned. A bearded hajji, who was quite proud he had made the pilgrimage to Mecca, entertained us with stories about the way Tangier used to be. He didn't emphasize its reputation as a gay resort, but he did mention William Burroughs, Allen Ginsberg, and others of the Beat Generation.

Our street parking spot proved to be such a convenient location we stayed there for a second night. Unfortunately King Hassan II was arriving the following day, so all the roads would be blocked along his route. Anyway, it was time to head for Lisbon.

"Why don't we leave from here?" I asked. "I'm not eager to see the hustler at that border again."

"Our return ferry tickets aren't refundable, so we'd lose money. But don't worry. We'll be on the other side of the divided road, so we won't have any contact with him."

On the drive to Ceuta, Bill promised he wouldn't try to reclaim our tear gas spray, and when we arrived, he hung back until the border crossing was clear before he drove in and quickly handed over our passports.

The young guard flipped them open. He held one up for inspection. He bent down for a closer look. Both of us looked straight ahead, not glancing at each other.

Without moving his lips, Bill muttered, "I think I made the wrong decision."

The guard scrutinized Bill again before motioning to someone. I didn't turn my head. I didn't want to know who was coming.

When his cohort arrived, the young guard pointed to Bill and said, "Keerk!" Then he repeated, "Keerk…Keerk Dooglass!"

When we drove off, I burst out laughing. "Bill, how could they think you look like Kirk Douglas? You don't have a dimple in your chin!"

10

CHINA: WE WEND OUR WAY

(Ina)

THE 1989 SCENES of Tiananmen Square's Cultural Revolution were played and replayed on TV. Bill wanted firsthand information. As he had exchanged lessons with several Chinese, he was ready to buy our tickets.

"We can't just hop over to a communist country without some planning." I insisted.

A month later we were standing on the deck of the ship we caught at Hong Kong Island peering through the fog for our first glimpse of Mainland China.

"Bill, listen to the organ music," I whispered.

Soft strains of "Amazing Grace" floated along the morning breeze. I didn't know it would prove prophetic.

On arrival at Guangzhou, Canton to us, I guarded our luggage while Bill went to call hotels. He returned with the two types of money we needed and Xiao, a young woman from Hong Kong.

"Xiao says hotels are booked solid because of a commercial fair, but she thinks she can get us a room where she's staying."

I hadn't had time to book hotels, and as their government mandates where we must stay, we gratefully accepted.

After her negotiation Xiao said, "I can get you a room if you're willing to wait until early afternoon."

We were willing. We expressed our gratitude and wishing her luck with her clothing booth, we promised to see her at the fair and went out to learn what was happening along the banks of the Pearl River. Though it was early, the city was already alive. Men stitched clothes on treadle sewing machines. Sidewalk barbers were either honing their straight razors or giving shaves, and in an open space near the river, men and women were practicing tai chi.

We attracted attention walking around, but when we sat on a bench and Bill held his language book—*Chinese without Pain*—with the title visible in both Mandarin and English, people stopped. Soon thirty or more were counting in Mandarin and then English. A few who knew the numbers were teaching me finger counting. For one through five I held up the appropriate number of fingers; eight was like a gun. I was working on nine when a police officer's whistle disbursed our group.

Bill said to the lone holdout, "Please ask him why I'm not allowed to teach. It's free."

The police officer's response was curt. It translated "Move."

We moved.

The holdout caught up with us with this warning: "Try not be see. Police no like groups."

"Try not be see" might have been good advice, but I was at a loss about how to camouflage Bill's blue eyes and my white skin and red hair.

At noon we walked around to see what others were eating. Pointing got Bill shrimp and rice, and I had watermelon soup served in the rind.

"Looks like we can afford to eat anything we like," Bill said after he paid the bill.

We both smiled at the young girl at the restaurant's exit, who bowed and thanked us for coming.

All the food we saw that first day looked tasty, and I was excited about trying new dishes. The next day we queued at the bus stop outside our hotel to go to a market my guidebook described as "worth going out of your way to visit." When the bus pulled up, the Chinese converged. Though we were first in line, we were the last to squeeze aboard. Waiting one's turn is obviously not de rigueur in China. I decided in a country with more than a billion people, each person must look out for himself. Once aboard I felt my arm clutched by a woman I thought looked older than I, and I was lowered into the seat she'd vacated. I suppose being nice to elderly foreigners was another of their ingrained habits.

Near the entrance to the market, Bill, who has never been accused of being prudent, was so taken by the exchange rate offered by an illegal money changer that he decided to change another fifty dollars. He asked me to go along to help him count. I followed him to a side street and watched the exchanger count out his *renminbis*.

They exchanged money and the man said, "Count again. Be sure is right."

While Bill was recounting, the exchanger shouted, "Police!" He shoved Bill's money back, snatched his renminbis, and took off on his bicycle.

I gritted my teeth, awaiting our second encounter with the police.

When Bill realized there were no police, he unfolded the corner of his bill. "Did you see him do this?" he asked. He held up a five-dollar note. "The fellow undoubtedly has tens folded the same way for greedier tourists. Anyone who can take me that easy deserves what he gets. But I won't be so gullible next time."

"You're going to be playing this game again?"

"Sure! This is Asia. I have to save face. I'm getting my forty-five dollars back."

Still discussing the fellow's sleight of hand, we entered the market, where stall after stall after stall contained heaping piles of dried, squashed, and shriveled black-and-red creatures. Insects? Lizards? Mice?

We watched vendors sliding these things into plastic bags. Others were pulverizing the "whatevers" with large stone pestles.

"They must be aphrodisiacs," Bill surmised. "Asians are big on them."

"If so, it's no wonder there are so many Chinese."

I wasn't surprised that the tanks of writhing snakes caught Bill's attention. Snakes fascinate him. They don't affect me that way so I left him for a look at a red fox, whose cage was so tiny I couldn't see all of him. I was on my way for a look at the dogs when my stomach began to churn. That red fox, those writhing snakes, the sad-looking hound, and the cute, fluffy little calico cat were on sale as…food!

"Of course they are," Bill said. "You read the Cantonese eat anything that flies except airplanes, anything in the water except boats, and anything with legs except tables."

"Well, from now on my pointing will be at words from your menu planner."

"Ina, we ate horse meat in France. That's the same as a dog or cat."

Bill had a point, but it took time before I looked at unfamiliar Chinese food with other than a jaundiced eye.

The giant pandas at the zoo were on my afternoon agenda. Bill joked, "I haven't seen you take any pictures of the giant pandas, but you've taken at least three of babies' bums."

"That's because the pandas keep hiding behind their bamboo shoots, but all the kids are on display."

I assumed because of China's one-child policy parents could afford to dress their children like little emperors and empresses. However, practicality took precedence when it came to the babies. The rear ends of their garments weren't stitched, making them ready to be held over trashcans for acts of nature. The Chinese toilet-train their children very early.

Infrequently spaced, low-wattage bulbs illuminated Canton's streets, making it difficult to navigate them in their torrential spring rains. But did we care? We were halfway around the world. Things shouldn't be as they are on our houseboat in Port Marly, France.

When Bill went to buy our boat tickets the next day, the price quoted was in renminbis, which translated "people's money." Foreigners were required to buy most things with FEC—federal exchange certificates. The ticket seller likely had no experience with Americans buying their own boat tickets, nor had we ever traveled seventeen hours for the equivalent of fifty cents.

Everyone on the dock seemed to be sitting on, or guarding, their big red-white-and-blue plastic bags. They looked us over as though we'd landed from outer space. "That lady over there seems to be counting the times I blink," Bill said.

When boarding time came, we crossed the sterns of three other boats to get to ours. We left our suitcases with the pile of their patriotic-looking sacks and located our places in one of the two layers of bunks that lined the boat's interior. Each bunk came with a thin, straw mat and a small, square pillow that felt like it was stuffed with pinecones.

"I'm glad I chose the top. It's the superior location," Bill said.

"You're right. So we should stake out our territory like everyone else."

Bill went to buy us the small hand towels the Chinese used to define territory. I got the hot-pink one with spring flowers. His had a lemon-yellow Donald Duck on a blue background.

"With these hanging on the ends of our bunks, we're sure to blend right in," he said.

Blend, we didn't. Bill again found himself under scrutiny by the blink-counting woman. She scrambled into the bunk next to his and exposed her two upper and three lower teeth with an engaging smile each time he looked her way.

"It's obvious that in addition to having an over-juiced libido, she's deranged," Bill told me before escaping to the outer deck. His lady friend followed. I smiled and wiped the dirty window with my hot-pink towel to watch the fascinating outside world.

Before it got dark, Bill insisted we trade places. "Then at least she'll have to climb over you to get at me."

We arrived in Wuzhou in the early morning and boarded the decrepit bus waiting to take passengers on the next leg of their journey. When we started up the first mountain, each grinding of the gears brought an ominous sound.

"I hope we can make it up these mountains for the next ten hours," I said.

"Ten hours!" Bill spluttered. "You didn't tell me this bus ride was ten hours."

"No, because you told me I could plan the trip, so I did."

Our trip was scenic. I saw the women carrying heavy loads on long poles balanced over their shoulders, rice paddies irrigated by bamboo pipes, and terrace upon terrace upon terrace climbing the steep mountainside. And up in these fields, blue-clad farmers turned the soil as their ancestors had done for thousands of years. In more modern scenes, their Russian tractors had engines almost twice as long as a John Deere and piglets were stuffed into elongated baskets, awaiting shipment to market.

Bill, always more interested in people than in scenery, was absorbed with his three-hour lesson with the young lady sitting opposite him. With the help of two dictionaries, he spent his time learning scenery-related words like *mountain, river,* and *plow.*

When we reboarded the bus after our lunch stop, almost everyone was chewing sugarcane. I had commented on the spitting prowess of the Chinese men in Canton. On this bus I got firsthand demonstrations that not just men, but also women had honed the skill. On arrival in Guilin, we made our way off the bus through all their sugarcane husks to be greeted by a horde of hawkers. Bill established a price, and the chosen one roped our luggage and transported us in his rickety, leg-powered vehicle to the "the very best and cheapest tourist hotel."

After registering, we bee-lined to a travel agency to sign up for the Li River trip—one of the top priorities on my sightseeing list.

"Do you hear these people grumbling about trains?" I asked Bill as we stood in line.

"No, but if they think they have it rough on trains, I could tell them about our marvelous boat and bus trip."

Had I listened, I wouldn't have slept well that night.

On our tour along the Li River, I couldn't understand our Chinese guide's English, but the German geologist sitting next to Bill explained it to me somewhat like this: Three hundred million years ago, this area was covered with water. During the next hundred million years, while the seabed was going up and down, the water dissolved some of the limestone and gypsum, which caused caves and sinkholes to form. Then around a hundred million years later, the water level fell, exposing all the formations.

A Chinese couple from Hong Kong then took over the job of retranslating our guide's English. They said the wind created all these unique karst shapes that we were seeing. Knowing the names of various limestone scenes didn't make them any easier for me to visualize. I had no idea what a "Yearning for Husband Hill" should look like. It didn't matter. The area was different from anything I had ever seen.

The couple also clarified the grumbling I'd heard about the trains. "Because there are so many tourists here now, the government just made a new law. Before anyone can book a train ticket to leave, they must first get official government permission."

I listened closely—my itinerary called for us to leave Guilin by train the next evening.

"We've been waiting four days," the wife continued, "so we'll probably get a train out by next Wednesday."

"But we can't stay that long," I said. "Three days is our absolute maximum."

"Oh, there are lots of things to do here. You should see the Thousand Buddha Cliff and take a bike ride to Reed Flute Cave and spend at least a day at the Seven Star Park."

"The Thousand Buddha cliff is on my list, but..." I repeated our time constraint. "Bill, if they speak the language, and they've been waiting four days, how long do you think it will take us to get out?"

The Germans had finagled a flight out that night, so Bill got their permission slips. The minute we docked, we took off for the train station. Bill presented the papers with numbers and stamps on them but was told "hard class" seats on an eighteen-hour train ride on Monday were the next available places. The train didn't go in the direction we were headed, but I said, "It might be a good idea to take it because it would at least get us out of here."

"I'm not sitting on a hard bench for any eighteen hours," Bill said. "This is no emergency."

"But by Monday we might consider it one."

"No way," he said, and we headed to the airport. After approaching every counter without success, he began haggling with the hustlers. For ten dollars extra, he bought two seats on a plane leaving for Chongqing early the next morning.

I had planned to see the countryside on the way to Chongqing from a soft-seat compartment on a train that took thirty-six hours.

11

China: Down the Yangtze on The East Is Red

(Ina)

The next morning our prop plane deposited us safely, if not smoothly. We took a pedicab to the wharf, and Bill went to buy our boat tickets to see the Three Rivers Gorge, purported to have some of the world's most spectacular landscapes.

Bill learned there were several classes of boats going down the Yangtze, not just the one I recommended. He returned, smiling over his two flimsy slips of paper. "I bought the best berths still available on one of their The East Is Red boats. The man said I could upgrade on board. I gave him an extra dollar so we can sleep on the boat tonight instead of looking for a hotel."

As Bill's bargain wouldn't allow us aboard until six o'clock, and with nowhere to leave our suitcases, we were confined to the small area around the dock.

Early on I made sure I'd learned two Chinese symbols—the ones that distinguished male toilets from female. The box head was for men. I also learned that stalls were almost nonexistent. In cities there were usually troughs to use, but a bale of hay spread in a dark shed sufficed in the country. In my short stay, I had already experienced several unusual toilets, but the one I found here was unique even among the extraordinary.

The toilet was crowded, but I thought I was in luck. There was an empty space at the very back of this tiled trough. I had strained my leg muscle, so squatting was difficult, but I straddled the channel and began my slow descent. Before I got stabilized, water gushed down. It hit with such force it knocked me forward. I sprawled on all fours—my wet bottom mooning the ladies. Again I hadn't followed the Canton boy's warning, "Try not be see." I berated myself. I should have known if there was an empty space anywhere in China, it was there for a reason.

Two females controlled their giggles enough to help me back on my feet. Someone else handed me a purple towel to dry off with, and I waited for a more appropriate place not under the sluicing jet.

Bill and I took turns walking around the dock. On my last quick inspection tour, I discovered several large, round, flat baskets filled with red chicken feet. They fit my new food criteria—meaning they were identifiable. I assumed the red color made them spicy. What I didn't know was whether they were to be swallowed or simply chewed and then spat out, like the sugarcane. With no time to wait for a demonstration, I left without buying one, so I had to add chicken feet to my list of culinary regrets.

Onboard, Bill found that The East Is Red fleet had no first-class accommodations, and the second-class cabins were booked solid—all three of them.

"Ten people in a room aren't so many," he insisted. "The boat you chose had more than two hundred."

"Yes, but we were on it only seventeen hours. Four days might make a difference."

It did. Our third-class bunks were again on the top, but this time it wasn't the choice position. Cigarette smoke from all eight of our Chinese professional male companions—three geologists, four engineers, and one professor—rose.

Their morning tooth brushing at the corner basin was so vigorous, it proved better than a shot of black coffee for getting me up and out. I liked being on deck, watching the sampans and junks as they navigated around us. The entire riverbank teemed with activity.

I provided entertainment—every time I tried to communicate, the cabin was transformed into a theater of mime. In exchange, when the boat moored, they guarded our possessions. Bill and I climbed up the bank into the town. After buying our favorite snack—fried, twisted dough sticks—we observed the countryside activities.

Bill began his cultural exchange on the first day aboard. Lessons with fourth-class travelers took place in a dormitory that housed a hundred. The steps between decks served as his classroom for those who slept in the corridors.

On the second day out, Bill said, "You might be able get some of the smoke smell out of your hair. The shower rooms are open."

Every time I went on deck, someone pointed to where Bill was teaching, so I held up my soap, shampoo, and hand towel, and a woman took me by the arm to escort me to the shower room. She knocked on the outside door; it remained locked. Not accepting defeat, she led me around to another door. After pounding, the door opened. I jerked back from the steam-filled-room, but she pushed me in.

There were two shower stalls with a steady stream of hot water coming from the overhead faucet. In front of the showers was a space for dressing, and along the walls were storage partitions—the shelves were so narrow my shoes would have toppled off had I tried to use one. With no idea how long it would take for the two adults already in there to shower the kids with them, but having learned not to wait around in China, I undressed, wedged my clothes in a cubicle, and stood there nude, my back to the showers.

Chinese curiosity wasn't long in asserting itself. Two kids ran up, stopped when they got even with me. They hesitated a moment before stretching their necks around to see what I looked like from the front. After they had a long look, they ran back, giggling. Was it my white skin or my red pubic hair that caught their attention?

Before long another pair made the journey for their peek. Each kid had at least one look before it was the adults' turn. Why I didn't turn around and save us all time, I'll never know.

The next day we would pass though the spectacular Three Gorges—the reason for this trip. A woman scooted others over so Bill and I could have a place at the railing.

For years I had taught sixth-graders about ancient China. They were attentive when I told them about the Chinese hurling their most beautiful young maidens into these raging waters while pleading with the river gods to keep the river from overflowing its banks and drowning thousands of innocent people.

Millions of years ago, when these mountains had also squeezed together, the pressure had caused faults in the area's limestone. Now torrents of water flowed through the fractures, forming incredible sights.

Organ music began playing over the loudspeakers as our boat maneuvered between the high, rocky cliffs and swerved around the hairpin curves.

The songs they were playing had no words, but I knew: *When them cotton balls git rotten, you don't git very much cotton.* I wondered if our song was an adaptation of an old Chinese air?

Bill's young students insisted we attend their dance on our last night aboard. We didn't expect to know the steps to their Chinese music, but we improvised. We both dance with more enthusiasm than skill, but who could tell in that dark, smoky room? Bill enjoyed dancing with two of his students, and the next morning at breakfast, one of the girls said, "You're a wonderful dancer, Bill."

Big-decision time came before we docked at Wuhan. With our two extra days, I favored making a detour to see the terra-cotta warriors at Xian. Bill wanted to take another boat to Shanghai, our next destination instead of the train.

"Ina, you know what those warriors look like. We saw a couple of them in Paris."

I'll always regret not getting to Xian to see them, but he shanghaied me.

This time our cabinmates purchased tickets for us. The East Is Red boat was more modern, and the group dynamic reversed—now there were nine females and Bill. One was a bride, whose traditional Chinese medicine company was sending her to a seminar. Her company wasn't paying for her husband to make the trip, which made me wonder why he was calling this their honeymoon, since he was sleeping in the hundred-person dormitory. He was an English interpreter, but his English was stilted-old-fashioned. His contacts were military representatives from other communist countries. Each day he sat on his wife's bunk, asking me the meanings and uses of our outdated jargon. I ran into trouble when I simply couldn't think of a way he might use "never on Sunday" in a technical discussion.

Then there was the afternoon of our style show. A French specialty store sent fabrics and designs to one of our cabinmates, and she provided the seamstresses. We ladies primped in front of our lineup of tiny makeup mirrors before we paraded down our cabin's improvised walkway in blouses sold under the French label Belle Boutique.

On the third day, Bill shouted when he hurried past our cabin, "We're coming into Shanghai."

When I arrived on deck, he was mesmerized, as near to the bow as he could get. No one can accuse Bill of being a camera tourist. The only activity he enjoys more than people watching is people talking, though that may come second if it competes with watching the activity at a large port. I guessed he was dreaming of living in an older Shanghai, fighting in one of the Opium Wars, or making a fortune in silk, guns, or tea.

We tied up at the Bund, the city's famous waterfront. Two of our cabinmates were so happy with their newly acquired English words that they insisted, to their husbands' chagrin, on carrying Bill's suitcase off the boat. My jargon man carried mine—eager, I'm sure, for the opportunity to say, "See you later, alligator."

12

China: Not Even a Smattering

(Ina)

"Bill, will you get us seats for the opera tonight?" I asked in an effort to pry him loose from the park bench across from our old art nouveau hotel. He was spending our days here exchanging lessons with the workers on lunch breaks, chess players, and men with birds in cages, but I wanted at least a smattering of culture in this most cosmopolitan of Chinese cities.

When he returned, Bill proudly showed me our tickets. They were for the circus. His explanation: "You wouldn't have understood a word at the opera."

Of course, he was right. I'm not even fond of opera.

At the circus we perched on a stadium bench, stupefied by balancing acts that made it appear people were lighter than air.

A Chinese friend in Paris had asked Bill to deliver some money, so he arranged a rendezvous. The recipient was most grateful, and over tea he had a good laugh at our misinterpretations of the many posters plastered on walls throughout the city. They were not most-wanted criminals, as we'd supposed, but pictures of the most-diligent workers in auto factory #1.

The fellow told us about their saying: "In heaven there is paradise, on earth Suzhou." The next day, we followed his recommendation to take a first-class train "to experience the now-faded elegance of travel from the time the French, British, and Americans had transformed Shanghai into an international city." The aroma of fresh flowers permeated our compartment. We relaxed in red, plush Victorian chairs, resting our arms on armrests covered with pristine antimacassars and our feet on the matching red footstools while we sipped tea from porcelain cups served by an elegant lady. For ninety minutes in China we were steeped in luxury.

At Suzhou's North Temple Pagoda, we climbed the long flight of stairs for a view of their famous canals and gardens.

"Yeah, it's a beautiful city," agreed Bill before he hurried back down to follow a bare-chested man straining to pull a flat cart stacked with what looked to me to be at least a ton of bricks. The man must have been in his late fifties and had probably been tugging that cart for years because his hemp harness had etched two deep scars into his shoulders. In spite of the load, his face had a tranquil expression, as though he got pleasure from pulling bricks. Although his body was bent, his legs moved like two powerful pistons.

Bill followed him for a block, murmuring, "Can you believe that? I'll never forget this man."

To entice Bill into a stroll down one of Suzhou's famed garden paths I used subterfuge. From experience I knew better than to quote the guidebook because if I mentioned flowers, Bill would do a repeat of his favorite—"Rocks may not have the scent of roses, but their texture and hidden colors are far more interesting"—so I said, "Let's go to the Lion Grove Garden. It has huge, eroded rocks that form caverns and grottoes."

We visited not only that one but three of the other gardens that had made the city famous. In the Humble Administrator's Garden, we were sitting in a sheltered nook intended for meditation when an excited couple from Xinjiang—the remote area where the Chinese tested their nuclear bombs—descended, waving a camera. First, they posed Bill with his arm around the bride. Then the groom put his arm around me.

"You don't think we were the highlight of their honeymoon, do you?" Bill asked.

The next day we took bus number four and found ourselves deposited in the middle of nowhere. But somehow even there our every move was observed, and an old man appeared. Bill's phonetic Chinese "Da Yunhe" (Grand Canal) led to a puzzled expression, so I used undulating hand movements and mimicked rowing. The old man pointed us in the right direction.

This longest canal in the world had been built because a Wu emperor wanted to deploy his troops rapidly. The canal wasn't remarkable to look at, yet when dangling our feet over the side and thinking about the thousands of conscripted coolies who had dug it, it became interesting. One of the sixty bridges along its path was here. It had a delightful name—The Precious Belt Bridge—and legend tells its name originated because a government official sold his precious belt to help finance its construction.

Our last stop: Beijing!

"Let's go to McDonald's," I suggested when we arrived. Their first restaurant had opened to rave reviews. After a month of eating unfamiliar fare, a hamburger had an almost magnetic appeal. But we missed this culinary delight, as we didn't want to wait in their long lines.

Instead my *Rough Guide* devoted several pages to "eating well on the cheap." We chose one of their recommendations at random and followed their instructions. We walked past the imposing entrance to climb the stairs located on the left, where we entered their "frill-free" room. So on our first night in Beijing, we feasted on Peking duck—the same food listed on the restaurant's posh menu—but we paid a fraction of the cost at this restaurant rated among the best in the world.

On Bill's list of must-sees was a museum with the world's oldest bronze artifacts. We climbed up many steps in Tiananmen Square to find it closed. Bill, unable to decipher the sign posted on the door, asked a young girl what it said. She explained, "It has been rebuked to the public!"

By chance we later happened upon another museum—a pay toilet. This marble underground structure overflowed with upright plants as well as hanging greenery reflected in gilded mirrors. When Bill bought our entrance tickets, Mama Pee Pee carefully unrolled and handed each of us two small sheets of toilet paper. She nodded to the young, uniformed attendant who escorted us to our own separate, private chamber, where he ceremoniously unlocked the doors.

When we exited, I sighed. "Ah!"

Bill agreed and added, "It topped any bronze pot I might have seen at that rebuked museum."

With our time running out, Bill resorted to changing small amounts of money to replace the forty-five dollars he'd lost in Canton. He employed a much safer black market method—he dealt only with those at small stands.

"Is only way," the bellboy in Guilin told him. "They no can run away."

Though we did make one trip on the subway just to satisfy our curiosity, we took a pedicab almost everywhere else we went in Beijing. Our swan song was to be a trip to the Great Wall, so we again followed *Rough Guide* directions and took the bus. We got off at the specified plaza, where Bill asked the people in a decorative, green wrought-iron kiosk for two tickets.

"Ina, are you sure we're in the right place?" he asked me after several minutes of fruitless efforts at conversation. "They don't seem to understand anything I'm saying."

I reread my directions. "Yes, we're in the right place," I assured him.

The more he repeated "*zài chángchéng*" (the great wall), the more bewildered their expressions became. Bill was getting nowhere. I wanted to walk on the Great Wall. "If you'll quit trying to speak Chinese, we can book with a tourist office," I said.

Bill kept trying so I walked off, hoping he would follow. He didn't. Around the corner I spied the kiosk that was selling the tickets and made our $1.25 purchase.

Bill smiled as he showed his new acquaintances what he had been trying to buy. They laughed and dragged out their brooms to let him know their kiosk held street-cleaning supplies.

The next morning I insisted we arrive early to ensure nothing went wrong. But since we were early, Bill took the opportunity to go buy the yogurt he liked. By the time he returned, the group had walked off, and I had no idea where our bus was located. I was ready to use a Chinese torture on him, but his time spent with the street cleaners paid off. One of them took my arm to escort us to the bus. It was evident they'd told the other passengers we needed looking after—at each stop someone pointed out on our watches when we should return—and throughout the day they gave us various snacks to sample.

We weren't interested in the places we visited before we got to the Great Wall. But there I paused by any groups I heard speaking English. When one guide mentioned that when coolies had keeled over from exhaustion, they became filling for the foundation, I began walking gingerly.

Our last stop was to be the Ming tombs. We were looking forward to them since we knew about the importance of the Ming dynasty. I was on the lookout for the triple-decked, triumphal arch that marks the entrance to The Spirit Way that leads to their tombs. The arch didn't appear. Instead our bus stopped by a statue of a reptile with cow horns. I reread my guide and realized this should have been the last statue we saw as we left.

So this trip was somewhat like my shower incident: we were to experience this last tourist sight with a look at the back before we saw the more interesting items in front.

13

USSR: To Moscow on the Trans-Siberian Express

(Ina)

WEDNESDAY MORNING WE arrived at Beijing's Zhan Railway Station to board the Trans-Siberian Express. I had booked us on the Chinese rather than the Russian train for this trip to Moscow for two reasons: it went through Mongolia, which I thought would be fascinating, and I'd read it served better food.

As I expected, our second-class compartment was compact. The shared bathroom, however, was a surprise. Though I hadn't expected I'd be luxuriating under a hot shower, I hadn't anticipated having to dance in and out of ice-water dribbles. But the variety of healthy potted plants was unexpected. Why potted plants? We hadn't a clue. Colorful ceramic pots covered the bathroom floor except for a small space in front of the lavatory and another in front of the toilet. We debated confronting the people with whom we shared the bathroom but decided not to bother. By stretching we could step over the plants. Fear that we might demand their removal was likely what kept our bathroom mates out of sight for the entire six days we were on the train.

Though the plants thrived with icy water, I didn't. Fortunately, a samovar with hot water for tea nestled on an open bed of hot coals at the front of each car. We didn't have teabags so I justified transporting its hot water for my sponge baths.

I hoped spotting a segment of the Great Wall would be the equivalent of throwing a coin in the Trevi Fountain—I so wanted to return.

At the border to Inner Mongolia, we made a prolonged stop for our Chinese train's wheels to become compatible with Russian tracks. Each of the heavy cars was lifted. Then, working by gaslights, a hefty crew removed the sets of wheels and installed ones the proper width.

Bill and I knew little about Mongolia, though I remembered teaching about Attila the Hun conquering and unifying the Mongolian tribes before turning west to devastate most of Europe. The kids liked the legends of his warriors chewing on raw meat heated under their saddles. I could quote two lines of Coleridge's poem: "In Xanadu did Kubla Khan / A stately pleasure-dome decree." And in Beijing we had sought out a restaurant that served Mongolian hot pot; the people at the next table had to show us the proper way to eat it.

I was afraid we might find out more about Mongolia than we wanted to know when the border officials came through checking passports. They also asked for our vaccination certificates.

"Bill, no one mentioned our needing vaccinations here."

Their "Where are your…?" countered by Bill's, "We don't have…" escalated. The officials finally stormed off.

Regaining his composure, Bill said, "Why did I do that? Those poor guys were just looking for some money. They probably don't make much. I should have put a couple of dollars in our passports."

"That would have been a good idea," I agreed. "Anyone who lives in a country where rancid yak butter is considered a delicacy deserves a little something extra."

I declined Bill's request to go with him to slip them a tip. I wanted to look for a yurt—one of the circular, domed felt tents where the nomads lived. I soon found there was little to see here. The scenery was dull—nothing but sand, sand, and more sand. Yet when Bill came back from his prolonged get-together, and needing to justify my selection of this train over the Russian one, I related a tale of seeing a band of warriors waving their scimitars as they charged around their yurts on wild horses.

"There was obviously some sort of hallucinogen in that tea you drank," Bill said.

"How could you possibly know what I saw? You were out in the hall *languaging*."

After our train left the sand of Mongolia, it rolled through Siberia. I spent my days reading *The Last Emperor of China* and looking out the window. I didn't bother to change my watch when we went through each of the seven time zones—where spring was either just budding or already blossoming, depending on the temperature. We rumbled across four rivers, including the Volga. I didn't hear any yo-heave-hoing from boatmen. Fortunately one traveler, who was an old hand at making the trip, alerted me in time to see the rather insignificant stone marker in the Ural Mountains, which delineates Asia from Europe.

Bill continued his lessons with the young Chinese steward, whose room was social headquarters. On several occasions Bill brought someone back to our cubbyhole. This was how I met the Chinese film producer whose direction of *Black Snow* had won first prize at the Berlin Film Festival. Usually my conversations were with people on our ramble to the dining room. Long before the dinner bell rang, we began making our way through the six intervening cars because Bill got waylaid for protracted conversations. On one of these stops, I met Sarah the psychic, who gave me her orange-and-orchid card with a PO box address in Honolulu. Tarot reading, crystal and holistic healing, and metaphysical writings were listed as her fields of expertise. She had gone to China to study horoscope reading to enhance her already-impressive résumé.

Bill kept trying to offer an "Allah Akbar" as we passed the bearded, eighty-year-old Mongolian trio en route to Mecca for the

Hajj, but he couldn't get their attention. They were either orienting their prayer rugs or reciting prayers. I wondered what they did if they were praying and the train veered, and they were no longer facing Mecca.

On our third night, after we were served yet more rather bland fare, Bill teased, "If the food on this train is significantly better than that on the Russian train, those people are in real trouble."

"And we could be drinking champagne and eating smoked salmon if someone hadn't been so wrapped up in exchanging lessons." The porter, who was running this scam, sold all his contraband stock before Bill got word of it.

Several travelers chose to make a stopover at either Novosibirsk, the capital of Western Siberia, or at Lake Baikal in Irkutsk, where they would spend four days until the next train passed. Bill's antics at Lake Baikal almost ruined our trip.

This stretch had only one set of tracks. Our train, the first to arrive at the lake, was shuttled off to allow the Russian train that would be arriving from the opposite direction to pass first. Russian soldiers took advantage of this prolonged stop to sell their military gear to the double sets of passengers. After Bill made his usual snack run, he stopped to bargain. He bought one military watch, but haggling for a second one dragged on. The train whistles blew. Bill made a final offer. With the deal completed, he sprinted for the train, but in his bargaining frenzy he'd forgotten which train was ours. As he caught the bar to climb aboard, a broad-shouldered Russian woman screamed, "*Nyet*! *Nyet*." If she hadn't blocked his way, I would have been exploring Moscow alone, while Bill would have had several days to compare the food on the Russian train.

We arrived in Moscow three hours late, so we hailed a taxi, deposited our luggage at the hotel desk—our rooms wouldn't be available until that evening—and hurriedly walked to the Bolshoi, hoping to buy last-minute ballet tickets. They were sold out, so Bill searched for scalpers. The contacts he made were with money changers. When he disappeared with one of them into a dark hallway, I worried, but minutes later he reemerged, unharmed, and with the promised amount of rubles.

As bilingual books "are practically given away in communist countries," according to Bill, he was torn between shopping and visiting Lenin's tomb. As Lenin's body was still undergoing its two-year reconditioning, I got to see most of the bookstores in Moscow. Fortunately I had been here before.

We staggered back to our hundred-dollars-a-night-room, the "must pay" price; otherwise Intourist wouldn't grant us visas. Bill closed the bathroom door firmly, hoping to block out the constant gurgling noises coming from the toilet.

I flopped on one of the unmatched twin beds to survey our Spartan accommodations. "Bill, we don't even have a view. There's just a solid wall facing us."

"But we're on the top floor. With no curtains on the windows, no one can view us either." He was right, and the bed was more comfortable than the one on the train.

The following day another train took us to Warsaw, where Bill booked our flight back to Paris. Before we landed in Germany, he learned there was an earlier plane, so he left me to guard his books and our hand luggage, while he went to cajole the ticket agent into transferring our luggage to this earlier flight. Bill accomplished his mission, but in so doing he forgot where he had left me. In all fairness Frankfurt is a large, complicated terminal.

"Ena Mahunee is urgently requested to report to gate number seventeen for immediate boarding." It took three repeats before I realized this heavily accented voice coming over the loudspeaker was referring to me.

So it was truly amazing that I managed to push a cart through the airport's maze and squeeze through the gate only seconds before it closed.

14

Thailand: Keeping Your Cool Is the Golden Rule

(Ina)

During the summer Bill began muttering about wintering in Bangkok. A month later he progressed to, "You know, their cool season begins in November."

"Bill, there is never a cool season in Bangkok. You must mean it's a fraction less hot." The thought of Thailand appealed, but we had to stay on board in winter—our furnace needed frequent prodding. Frozen water pipes and boats do not interact well together.

In November our furnace died. We had a new one installed. So two weeks before Christmas, we landed in the Land of Smiles, in the middle of their month-long celebration of the king's birthday. Added to the lights strung all over the city for him were artificial Christmas trees with cotton balls simulating snow—the sole reminder of winter weather.

We both enjoyed noisy, dirty Bangkok; the tuk tuks racing through the streets and the night markets filled with everything imaginable ensure the city is alive at all hours. But to avoid some of its pollution during the heat of the day, we liked to spend as much time as possible near the Chao Phraya River—Thailand's equivalent of the Mississippi.

On our first full day, Bill asked the young girl on our air-conditioned bus where to get off to catch the river express. She told him, "Finish way." So, at the end of the bus route, we boarded the ferry for a trip upriver. The Chao Phraya teemed with activity—many boats zipping by, and kids diving and swimming by their houseboats.

On our way back, we stopped at the Sheraton Hotel to hear a local girls' high school choir. Their singing, "Oh, Night De-Wine" lent a special meaning to this Yule season.

The Thai way with words charmed us. Who wouldn't feel like celebrating after being wished "Happy jingle bells!" or realize their comfort was of foremost importance after reading this sign posted in a hotel: "We ask our custrom not to open the windows because of a cricket's invasion, which are harmless animals but noisy." And when we read "salad of chicken ankles in lemon butter" on a menu, neither of us could resist ordering a plate of ankles.

The day Bill stopped to have a lesson in the park by Thammasat University, I watched a kite fight. By pulling various strings, one young man was making his dragon twist and lunge in dogged pursuit of a queen bee. But queenie recovered in time to make a stunning swoop, cutting his line and winning the contest.

Bill's student must have noticed my interest, because he offered to take us to a fighting fish match. "Two males put in same tank but separated by piece of cardboard. When cardboard pull up, fish color change. Go from white to bright red before begin life or death fight!"

I would have enjoyed seeing the color changes, but watching a fight, especially to death, had no appeal. So why I agreed to accompany Bill to Lumpinee Stadium to watch kickboxing remains a mystery. I hate boxing. I think it's barbaric, and calling it a sport a gross misnomer.

For this occasion Bill settled for nothing less than the best seats, so we sat ringside with the other *farangs*—a word I thought translated as "white-skinned foreigners." I learned that to many Thais it meant "fair-skinned foreigners with hearts that are liable to overheat." I appreciated the pageantry of the opening ceremony, the stylized religious dancing and praying designed to loosen the boxers' muscles, but when the kicking and punching started, I turned my head. This was when I discovered the gamblers standing in an open space a few rows behind us. While waving their fistfuls of bahts, they screamed and ranted, changing bets after telling blows.

The Thai psyche is "a puzzlement." Earlier we had stopped to watch a young Thai scolding the drunk driver who had demolished his new motorcycle; he never raised his voice, yet I suspected that if he'd attended this match, he would have been as bloodthirsty as the rest of that screaming mob.

In return for his night of mayhem, I asked, "Will you help me locate a store I read about on my first trip to Bangkok? They sold dinosaur turds."

Bill agreed, "Yeah, one will be a good conversation piece for the ledge in our entrance room."

We kept a hodgepodge collection there: myrrh from Yemen, Stone Age flint knives from Belgium, an incense burner, seashells, and what Bill said was a two-million-year-old fossil.

The store was no longer listed in my guidebook, but I remembered its general location—two blocks from the central post office where we picked up our mail. We located it eventually. The prices listed on their displays had to be the reason it was no longer under "good buys in Bangkok."

"Let's not bother going in."

"I got black lungs looking for this place, so I'm seeing what they have," Bill said.

Fossils have always intrigued him, and the salesgirl showed him their extensive collection of dinosaur turds. She turned on infrared and black lights so we could peep in the shadow boxes that held them. The blue light she shone on one fossilized excrement caused it to sparkle. Bill became enamored. It took effort to convince him it was far too big to fit on our window ledge. Since it cost five times what I'd expected, we left without even a small turd.

Trekking was a major topic of discussion among the backpackers with whom Bill talked. They convinced him we should make the effort to see how the numerous Thai Hill Tribes lived, so off we went north to Chiang Mai, trekking headquarters.

After an eighteen-hour train ride, this ancient city with some of its original ramparts greeted us with three-foot lights blinking the New Year greetings. Thais celebrate their own beginning of the year on the anniversary of Gautama Buddha's death—543 BE (Buddhist Era). At this water festival, they first give his statues a bath before drenching each other. Water descends from buckets thrown from balconies and is sprayed from hoses, or thrown from any handy container. On a previous visit we were prime targets twice, thoroughly soaked, but in that climate we dried quickly.

The Thais want to be good enough to be reborn to a better life, but I've often thought they may want to enjoy this life even more. They'll cheer on the dragons that parade through the streets to usher in the Chinese New Year. They'll send syrupy valentines in February—though they don't display affection openly—and they find an occasion to celebrate something in each of the other months.

While looking for trekking information on our guesthouse's bulletin board, Bill read, "The Westerners who are in the jail will appreciate a visit over the holiday."

"Ina, we need to go there."

Prisons intrigue Bill. I've always assumed this stems from his ten-day confinement in juvenile detention.

As there were no Americans on the roster, he asked to see the Canadian. Not knowing Jules Beaudet presented no problem. Seven prisoners were ushered in and stood behind a grilled fence—Jules was the sole Caucasian. A five-yard barrier separated us, so it took effort to learn he owned a yacht moored at Ko Samui, where he and his friends were diving instructors. We didn't ask; we just assumed his charge was drug related. Shouting doesn't make for confidence sharing.

The guards took the chocolates and cigarettes we'd brought but wouldn't allow more than two of the C batteries. "Danger of making an explosive" was their reason.

A man who represented one of the Christian churches made eye contact with Bill and nodded toward his pocket. Bill slipped him the batteries to deliver later.

With the prison visit over, trekking was again the topic of interest to Bill. Most backpackers recommended their trek as The Ultimate Experience. They went "farther into the hills, deeper into the jungles, or higher into the mountains." And only they had discovered "authentic, never-seen-before villages."

The more I heard, the less enthralled I became. I wasn't about to go deep into any jungle, and I didn't intend to take malaria tablets. Admitting either wouldn't impress Bill, so I tried, "We'll be nothing more than voyeurs walking into their villages. They'll find it degrading to be stared at by strangers."

He was quick to answer. "They're willing for people to see how they live. It gives them opportunities to sell their crafts."

I convinced him we should go back to Bangkok where there was more to do and make a trekking choice next year after we had more information.

(Bill)

When we returned Ina had a letter from her mother. She decided her mother needed her, so she flew to Texas. That was when I began what was to become my yearly Bangkok cultural exchange.

I took my credentials to the campus policeman at Thammasat—one of the best universities in Thailand—to ask if I could exchange free lessons there. He told me, "This is a public place" and suggested I use one of the tables outside the English Department.

I began helping a student write articles for the *Bangkok Post* and others with their various assignments. Each day during lunchtime, a lady in her fifties walked by and stared with an unmistakable expression of displeasure. Our frequent laughter must have given the impression we were having a party rather than lessons.

"She's my teacher and head of the English Department," Silipon, one of my students, whispered.

Mrs. Happiness clearly believed proper decorum was necessary for learning. On the third day, she informed me I was on private property. "Take down your sign and go."

I tried to explain my purpose, but she ordered her students to leave and walked away.

I went to her antechamber. Her secretary listened while I explained that I considered free language lessons a worthwhile activity. So if I wasn't welcome, I wanted her to tell me why.

"Oh, of course you're welcome," the secretary said with typical never-say-no Asian cordiality. "Only she says you can't stay."

"Then may I speak with her, please?"

Her demeanor told me that here, as in France, the boss is God, and her only option was to obey. Remaining courteous yet persistent, I waited.

She looked toward the director's door before quickly writing a name and building address. "Talk to him," she whispered as she slipped me the note.

In this office, Number-Two-Man-on-Campus greeted me cordially. He examined my credentials and asked me to unroll my sign. After he identified the languages scripted in Chinese, Arabic, Korean, Japanese, and Hebrew, he said, "I feel sure there'll be no problem. Where would you like to conduct lessons?"

"Where most students pass."

He photocopied my passport and asked me to leave my sign. The next morning I was delighted to see it hanging in the area outside the administration building. The tables there were the most impressive on campus. Each had a bronze plaque with the name of a famous alumnus. When I went to express my gratitude, he showed me the information he had posted on all the department bulletin boards. It explained both my activity and location.

Teaching enthusiastic students was fun, but when it came to exam time, I switched from academia to Bangkok by night.

I set up on Soi 13 a street that intersects Sukhumvit Road, one of Bangkok's main thoroughfares. Competition for the table nearest the sidewalk was fierce. The first night I placed my open manila folder on this table—the language info written on front and back—to attract foot traffic.

Expats tried to own this spot. Ray, a huge, blond former Aussie rugby player who would have made a good union agitator, orchestrated the comments about the chutzpah of the pushy Yank muscling in on their territory. He was big enough to remove me with the ease of a junkyard crane, so I kept my mouth shut and my eyes on the passing traffic—and arrived each night before he did.

The first time a middle-aged Thai lady came up and held out her hand, I assumed she was begging. I learned that because of my large, ancient-looking, black leather-bound book, illiterates think I'm a Nostradamus.

My weirdest acquaintance was a black-haired woman in her late forties who neither drank nor smoked. The regulars said for the past ten years, she had come nightly to sit on the same stone steps in front of the tailor shop, wearing the same black dress; a large, silver owl brooch above her right breast; and matching silver shoes. She must have been quite attractive in her youth—her figure wasn't bad, and her complexion was still lovely. Yet there was a mysterious air about her.

She told a story that never changed: "I married an Austrian millionaire, but I left him. He regularly drives by my place in a limousine with smoked glass windows just to steal a glance at me, though he knows I'll never take him back."

Another Thai lady begged me to write a letter to the British embassy. She showed me a picture of her holding a bowling ball high in the air. She said she had won first prize in a tournament five years earlier and wanted the embassy to force the English bank sponsors to pay her the £2,000 prize money they had promised. I wrote her letter to Mr. The Ambassador. Before leaving she squeezed my shoulders, and swore she'd share part of her winnings the moment her check arrived.

15

Thailand: Down the River on a Bamboo Raft

(Ina)

By Christmas, I had my recommendation ready if Bill insisted we go trekking. Mrs. Thip's Adventure Tour featured a visit to her Lisu village. It wasn't deep in any forest where I would need malaria pills. I was counting on her raft trip down the Kok River to catch Bill's attention. It did, so we flew directly to Chiang Mai, and from there we would take a local bus to catch the tour at nearby Tha Ton.

"Bill, I don't think those shorts are appropriate travel clothes."

An elderly Buddhist monk sitting across the aisle from us kept looking at Bill's exposed legs. After a few minutes, he reached over to give the leg hairs a gentle tug.

Bill laughed as he told me, "He's just curious because Thais have little body hair."

Whatever his reason, the monk's smile as he pulled was angelic.

The next morning we joined our two young companions—Tonya, a Canadian; and Antonio, an Italian—on our "newly constructed bamboo raft made exclusively for you." As Chow, the captain; and Nan, his helper, began steering us around the many bends of the

Kok River, I kept checking to see if the white stone Buddha, positioned high on a hilltop to keep watch over the countryside, still had us in view.

The middle section of our raft had a thatched roof, so it served as our sitting area, dining room, and bedroom. The toilet hung over the water on the side. On my first trip there, I opened the bamboo door and saw two extra-large bamboo poles with a space between them. I placed a foot on each pole, swiveled to slip the rope loop back over the post to hold the door in place, and stood for a moment, watching the river flow underneath me. The design was quite workable. Bill declared, "It's ingenious!" Though Tanya confessed she'd be too embarrassed to use it. I didn't understand how she could travel in Asia and retain such modesty. After our first meal, I was afraid she'd have no choice.

Nan set up a clay charcoal brazier near his aft station to grill chicken while he kept up his steering. When we finished lunch, he leaned over to wash our dishes in the river. Either the fast-moving current cleansed itself, or we had all traveled enough to acquire immunity to the less-virulent bugs, as no one came down with *Thai tummy*. Tanya preserved her modesty.

That afternoon Nan tied up our raft, and we waited for Asa, Mrs. Thip's nephew, to trek us through the nearby forest. He pointed out litchi trees, banana blooms, and other flora, and he took us by a spring where string bags and tin cans served as containers to hold eggs that were cooking in the hot, sulfurous water.

When we arrived at the entrance to the Akha village, Asa said, "Look at the carvings on their ceremonial entrance gate. Notice the airplanes, cars, and bicycles. They are meant as warnings to the spirit world that only humans are allowed to come to this village."

The Akha migrated here from Tibet two thousand years ago, but as they had been slow in changing their traditional ways, they ranked as one of Thailand's poorest Hill Tribes. We stopped in their open courtyard to watch a young girl husking rice. With her foot she tapped one end of a long bamboo pole propped up at an angle. Her lethargic movements caused the stone attached to the other end of the pole—with an attached cord—to drop into a shallow depression. After around fifty taps, she had removed the husks from a half-cup of rice.

Their houses were built on stilts, and pigs wallowed in the mud underneath them. As with most Hill Tribes, their headgear identified their tribe. I didn't see anything they'd spent money on except their colorful, ornately beaded helmet-type hats. One woman, with beads woven around her silver coins, invited us to come up on her porch to examine her crafts.

After we left, Bill asked, "Why did you get that ugly shoulder bag? There are lovely ones in the market."

"I felt obliged. You said these people were willing to be stared at to make money. All four of us did a lot of staring, and no one else was buying anything."

Just before dark we joined Mrs. Thip's much-more-prosperous Lisu patriarchal clan, which had also migrated from Tibet. Her niece had learned meal preparation for foreigners in Bangkok and served us a delicious curried chicken. Her father, who looked about eighty, was missing most of his teeth. He entertained us by accompanying himself with various stringed instruments and spirited tribal dancing.

Our beds were on a raised wooden platform built over a dirt floor. I was so cold, I'd have sworn I didn't get any sleep, but that couldn't have been true because loud blaring rock and roll music woke me early in the morning. We all waited our turn at their outdoor communal toilets before huddling around a smoldering log to eat a breakfast of fruit and toast spread with pineapple jam. Bill eyed Asa's father, who kept opening a metal container and digging out a white paste to spread on the leaves he was gumming.

"So that's where he got his energy last night," Bill whispered.

"But I thought Asa said his tribe doesn't use drugs," I replied.

"I think he said they don't *sell* them."

"Oh."

After we looked around the village—which was of a much higher class than the Akhas—we trekked into a town to attend a hotly contested competition held in the town square. One team of seven players flipped dinner plate-size tops into a circular area drawn in the dirt. The opposition then spun their tops, endeavoring to either hit or force the first tops out of the circle. The rivalry became as intense as Thai kickboxing.

When we went back to our raft, Nan had spread out a sheet of plastic for us to sit on. I was puzzled as to why because when we passed elephants splashing themselves with water as they took their baths, the river remained calm. I got my answer when we hit our first rapid, though it was mild compared to the wake left by the "longtails"—the powerful boats that had gotten this name because their drive shafts had been lengthened to keep their propellers underwater. Most of the motors were converted automobile engines, so they were powerful.

Rafts keep well away from these longtails, but Tanya was out of vacation time, so she had to be let off. As we approached the dock, Nan called out, "Hold on tight!" I grabbed for the bamboo pole that supported the roof. The wake of one of the longtails whizzing by caused us to rock crazily—somewhat like the carnival rides I enjoyed as a kid. "The Buddha on the cliff is doing his job," I said when we eventually settled down.

That afternoon we tied up on a sandy bank. Nan threaded chickens on long sticks and cooked them over our campfire. I went to bed under the net I'd brought along, leaving the men alone for some guy talk.

Bill told me later, "Nan had difficulty, but finally got through to Antonio.

"He laughed and said, 'Oh, no, I have a girlfriend back home.'"

"Nan didn't think having a girlfriend was reason enough to ignore Tanya's interest."

On our arrival in the city of Chiang Rai, we watched with a bit of nostalgia, while Chow and Nan dismantled our home. They would sell the bamboo for a hundred bahts, around three dollars, before returning on a longtail to build another "newly constructed bamboo raft made exclusively for you!" and make their three-hundredth-plus trip on the Kok River.

On our way to Bangkok Bill said, "The reason we had to disembark so often to sign a register was two tourists were recently killed in an attack on a raft. Both Nan and Chow said they were especially careful because, 'If you get killed like them, we go to jail.'"

(Bill)

When I got to Soi 13 for my month alone in Bangkok, the tailor on the corner greeted me. We would practice English and Thai phrases and at eight o'clock when he pulled down his grille for closing, he'd let me hang my sheet. Noi, my Chinese waitress friend, would set up her twelve tables. She'd place the table nearest the sidewalk last so I could put my language folder where it could be seen from both directions. I left another sign with Sim Chai, the boy who sold brochettes from his pushcart. If I happened to be late, he put it on the table to reserve my place.

Around ten o'clock "girls," aged fifteen to thirty, began arriving in taxis. Others would come on the backs of "motos," sitting sidesaddle. They gracefully dismounted, every coiffed strand of hair still in place. Another group came after other bars around Bangkok closed. Most wore short skirts and high heels. Their destination was the nearby infamous Ther Mae Tea Room. No name could be more incongruous. It was located in the basement of a hotel complex only recently renamed the Clinton Plaza.

Pilots, doctors, journalists, lawyers, businessmen, and retired military men from age twenty to over seventy came to the tearoom to meet the girls. The place was packed until three in the morning but remained open until five. Many of the girls earned enough to support children or elderly family members.

I had brief lessons, but considerable conversation with these girls. They told me about their childhood tragedies and tales of close friends succumbing to AIDS. One showed me her wrists—she had slashed them three different times. Some were high on amphetamines or whatever else kept them going. Most came from Issan, a poor area in the north. Some went back occasionally to see their parents, but few fulfilled their dreams of returning.

I frequently saw a hunchback guy from New Zealand, who had to be pushing seventy, walk by hand in hand with an attractive teenager.

One of the regulars, who would stop by my table if he left the tearoom without a girl, told me about two seventeen-year-olds there who were so gorgeous, if they made an appearance on a London stage, flitting around bouncing balloons, they'd earn a thousand dollars. Here they went to bed for twenty or thirty dollars. One night he stopped to complain about "all the good stuff being taken early." He added, "You must have seen the beauty I waltzed by with last night."

16

THE US OF A

(Ina)

WHEN I RETIRED, I promised Mother I'd see her at least once a year. She thrived on challenges, so preferred visiting us where she not only made great suggestions, but she wielded a hammer or a needle and thread to carry out her recommendations.

On one visit she handed me her sterling silver flatware. "I don't entertain much anymore, so these will go well with your Rosenthal china. It'll dress up your dining table."

"Mother, the entertaining we do doesn't warrant your silverware."

"But you tell me about the lovely dinners your friends invite you to. I certainly hope you're doing your share of entertaining in return."

Since I can't compete with any French cook, I serve Tex-Mex food—dishes they don't know a great deal about. "At our dinners," I confessed, "we have to keep reminding our friends that tacos are finger food and not eaten with a knife and fork."

I didn't tell Mother my dinner's success was due to Bill's big pitcher of margaritas.

This summer Mother's health wouldn't allow her to visit us, so we flew to Texas. Instead of making it a there-and-back trip, we planned to see some of our own country. Within a week of our arrival, Bill bought a three-year-old, gray Ford pickup truck with a vinyl top. The advertised "California interior" provided bins along the length of each side for our clothes, and a carpeted floor served as our bed. With one cooking pot, a one-burner propane stove, a troubleshooting light on a long cord, a fan, and an ice chest, we were ready to make a first loop through the South.

Mother warned us, "You'd better not go through Louisiana. It's still raining, and there's already so much water, crocodiles and poisonous snakes are swimming in the ditches!"

Before we kissed her good-bye, I crawled through the sliding panel between the cab and the back to demonstrate that I wouldn't have to get out in inclement weather, and Bill assured her he would keep a sharp eye out for crocodiles and snakes. I had no need of his assurance; I knew he would, just not in the way she meant.

At the Louisiana border and all subsequent borders, we stopped for their free maps and brochures. With my yellow Magic Marker, I connected some of the scenic routes with a few other places. *Voilà*—our itinerary!

Aren't mothers always right? At least mine is. In Louisiana many roads were flooded. And true to his promise, Bill watched for snakes and crocodiles. He saw a small croc in a ditch. Naturally he stopped for a better look.

"I'm gonna see what he'll do when I wave this branch." Thankfully it swam off before he could find out.

One of the café waitresses said, "A snake slithered up into our toilet this morning. It was small and wasn't a venomous water moccasin."

Even so, I became more cautious.

By noon each day, we were ready to eat our big meal of the day. If we stopped for Chinese food, Bill got blank stares when he tried Mandarin—staff in most Chinese restaurants speak Cantonese. He used Spanish whenever possible. We took advantage of the seafood, sharing crawfish tails with the laid-back, straw-hatted bayou folks. Their ancient French amused Bill, and he listened for words no longer used in France. Along the way I introduced him to a lot of good ole Southern home cooking. With our glasses of sweetened ice tea, we ate lots of chicken-fried steaks, black-eyed peas, collard greens, catfish, and more kinds of cornbread than I knew existed.

Southerners taught us how to push our glasses against the dispenser when we wanted ice from the machines—a skill we hadn't needed in France. When a grocer asked, "Paper or plastic?" I replied, "But I've already paid."

He laughed. "I know, honey. I'm asking what kind of bag you want me to put your groceries in."

There are lots of things any tourist has to learn about a country—in our case even our own country.

Some nights we spent in state or national forests or parks. Otherwise Bill was skillful at finding substitute places. "No one will question us being in this hospital parking lot." We opted for a commercial campground when we needed to use a washing machine.

The inner area of New Orleans—pardon me, it's "N'awlins"—was roped off for a grand prix-type race. Bales of hay protected all the street corners. It was thrilling when the cars roared past. My pulse rate jumped, and the buildings seemed to vibrate.

After the race Bill drove to a public square where he warned, "It's dangerous leaving a car unguarded in this crime-ridden city!"

Then he left to visit the French Market, hoping to locate the building where he'd slept and run errands for gamblers when he was fifteen—they had let him sleep there in return for his keeping them supplied with sandwiches and tobacco.

Bill had gone a block before he returned, "Roll up the windows and keep the doors locked."

I might be safer, but he was out of his mind. The temperature was already 89 and I felt sure it would soon be 95.

When Bill was out of sight, I rolled down the windows, but soon after, I gave up, started the motor, and turned on the air-conditioning.

When he came back from his search he said, "My warning to you proved prophetic. On my way back, a young fellow crossed the street and approached me. Suspecting he might try to rob me, I reached for my coin blackjack. He must have picked up on this, as he moved on without confrontation. I walked a few more blocks before I heard sirens and turned to see the same guy flash by in a red Pontiac, a police car in hot pursuit."

I told Bill, "I heard sirens. I saw the car. It was headed straight toward me. The door was locked, so I couldn't get out fast enough. I was sure it was going to hit me, but it careened around the corner, and the police car skidded around behind it."

I shifted into gear and drove off.

Bill isn't into silence. While I enjoyed the scenery, either one of his language tapes was instructing him to "Repeat this phrase…" or the radio was imploring us "to repent of our sins or risk hellfire and damnation." These evangelical radio preachers entertained Bill. He was upset when he couldn't find a pen to copy down the address to send for the crucifix that glowed in the dark or the pink handkerchiefs blessed by Reverend Gospiter, which he wanted to take to Michel.

On our way back from Key West, Bill mentioned we should go snorkeling. Snorkeling? Me? From long experience he knew I would never consider putting my face in the water. I swam surveying everything in front of me. Nevertheless, the next morning at six o'clock, I gladly boarded a boat along with a dozen others for a half-hour ride to an offshore, underwater Paradise, longing for a few quiet hours.

Before we got to our destination, Bill began, "This is a chance of a lifetime! You must see the sea life this place is famous for…"

To keep from hearing more, I donned the life jacket and the snorkeling equipment. I hung the laminated card—designed to help me identify the multicolored fish—around my neck. I planned to get in the water, but return to the boat when Bill became otherwise occupied. And though my mind knew the life jacket would hold me up, it still took willpower to trust it. I stared down and leaned over a few times before I could force myself to slide into the Gulf of Mexico. I moved my arms frantically but then slowed my movements when I discovered how easy it was to stay up. To speed

Bill on his way, I called out, "I'm OK. This is easy," waggling good-bye with my fingers.

When I realized he wasn't going to leave, and desperate for some quiet time, I cautiously lowered my face into the water. I saw a blue, sharp-snouted fish chasing a yellow striper, while a school of sleek silver fish darted around below them.

I have no idea how long Bill monitored me. I was too absorbed in the magic of this underwater paradise.

This was one time Bill had to listen to me detailing the fish I had identified.

In Sarasota, Florida, nostalgia again overtook Bill as he recalled another of his youthful adventures. This time it took help from a University of Florida publication to locate the Muckland Celery farm.

I listened as he rehashed this story he'd written—though I could quote it almost as well as he, as I had typed and retyped it several times.

"That job lasted three weeks. I was the only male and the only white who worked the four-to-midnight shift. My domain was on the second floor of the warehouse in the middle of celery fields.

"Around eleven o'clock the lovely black ladies would sing Old Man River. I was plenty tired by that time, but when *he just keeps rollin'* came risin' up, I unfolded those celery crates and slid them down like the shift had just begun.

"I received smiles from some of the forty inspired ladies, their mouths opened wide, their white teeth flashing, their vocal cords vibrating the rafters and making me religious happy. While the floor, my body, and the whole building hummed, I looked down at the glorious quilt of blue, red, and yellow polka dot dresses swaying gracefully, as the women filled crates from the mountains of green celery and white ice.

"Each night I made contact with a soul who made me feel she was singing just for me. When she smiled and I heard 'He must know something,' we both knew we were communing with our Maker."

On the evening we spent at Tootsie's Orchid Lounge in Nashville, I listened to endless "somebody done somebody wrong" songs. My early exposure to country music hadn't made me appreciative of nasal twangs. Again Bill was in great form, singing along with these musicians who dreamed of joining the Grand Ole Opry stars who'd been discovered at Tootsie's.

We made our way back to Texas by way of the historic Natchez Trace.

This fascinating jaunt through the South added to our appreciation of our good old US of A.

Before we began our tour of the West, Mother was ready with yet another of her cautions. This time it was, "There have been a lot of road rage shootings in California, so you'd better not drive like you do in France." Shaking her finger at Bill, she said, "Don't you take Ina Ruth into that Los Angeles neighborhood where they had the terrible riots a few years ago."

We both assured her we knew American driving habits were very different from those of the French. "We would never play their game of cutting anyone off," I promised her.

Then before Bill could say anything, I added, "I'm sure Bill wouldn't think of taking me into a dangerous area." I managed saying it with what sounded like conviction.

Bill thought the "ro-Day-oh" we saw in Cheyenne was as exciting as the ro-De-o in Fort Worth. I agreed.

We drove through Napa Valley to compare it to the wine-growing regions in France. It was every bit as interesting. And the Redwood National Forest is in a league by itself. It made me feel as though I were in a sacred place.

We did two more of Bill's nostalgic tours—one to the UCLA campus and another to where he'd taken part in the creation of the Purple Sage Camp in the hills above Malibu. He and friends had built a corral and cleared a lot of land. Now a Japanese college, with stone gardens and pools with names like Meditation Garden and Willow Tree Pool, was in its place. An impressive Hindu temple stood to the right of the camp's entrance.

Of course we were given a chance to buy drugs.

Bill had run a rooming house in the Lake Wood area when he attended UCLA. He wanted to go by this house on the way to buy a Bible in Korea Town. When we drove by the lake, several males standing along the near-by streets shaped their hands like they were pointing a gun.

"Bill, get out of here fast!" I said.

Later, when he went to buy the Bible he asked the proprietor if he knew the area. "Yes," he said, "but I wouldn't go near that place. It's a crack area controlled by Central Americans. They were signaling you to buy."

We spent our last week with Bill's daughter, Sharon, and her family in Ukiah, California, and made plans for their visit to our boat in Paris. We left our truck with her husband, Ralph, to sell.

This was another of those occasions when I questioned why I'd stayed away so long. I love my country and people, and Bill feels Route 66 and his hitchhiking days are part of his bloodstream.

17

Thailand: More Jingle Bell Encores

(Ina)

Our raft trip down the Kok River fueled Bill's enthusiasm. His desire for trekking was quenched, but he still thirsted for knowledge about Thailand's nonurban population. Once again, at Christmas, we landed in Chiang Mai. Soon after our arrival, a local bus took us near Mae Salong, a town settled by Chinese nationalists. After Mao's communists took over China in '49 most nationalists chose to settle in Taiwan, but one group came to this mountainous hideaway.

Though the taxi driver Bill hailed might have driven up this mountain daily, I didn't think this qualified him to see around bends. As he screeched his old cab around the uphill curves, unmindful of oncoming traffic, I dug my fingernails into Bill's leg and shouted, "Our wheels are on the edge of the road. We're going to go over the cliff!"

After Bill said, "This nut is getting his confidence from either alcohol or drugs," I wanted to shout, "Stop! Let me out!"

I arrived badly shaken. After we got settled the proprietor of our guesthouse suggested we visit the Hill Tribes' weekend market.

We went, but I didn't shop. I was too busy sneaking peeks at the women's necks.

When a daughter in the Padaung tribe turns six, her parents begin putting brass rings around her neck. As she grows they add more. Eventually, the weight of a dozen or so heavy rings crushes the girl's collarbone. Without the collarbone, a neck looks at least a foot long.

"Let's rent horses," Bill suggested.

Mine was a rosinante whose ribs showed through her gray, unbrushed hide, but she and I ambled along contentedly. Bill passed the same cherry trees we did. He rode through the same fields of coffee and tea, just at a much faster clip.

He stopped to watch school kids line up to greet their teacher. They put their hands together, placed them under their chins, and ducked their heads to perform the *wai*, the gracious Thai greeting. "Why didn't our students show that kind of respect?" he asked when my horse ambled up beside him. He was out of sight, so he didn't see them later making faces and cavorting, just as most kids would.

"The nationalist army brought in enough weapons to begin a thriving business in the drug trade," Bill complained. "Mae Salon looks more like Hong Kong than rural Thailand."

He wanted something more rustic than a glut of television sets, Walkmans, and bicycles.

A more conservative driver, recommended by the owners of our guesthouse, drove us down the mountain where Bill signaled a *songthaew*, an open-sided truck used in rural Thailand. The driver threw our backpacks on top. (After our trip to China, we realized backpacks were more practical than suitcases.) We crawled into the truck and took the last two places on the benches located along the sides. Down the road, when five new arrivals couldn't be squeezed in, the driver slid in a spare bench he kept on the roof.

A Hmong woman holding her baby now sat across from Bill. I found myself knee to knee with her fierce-looking husband. He was dressed completely in black and his loose-fitting trousers were gathered at the ankles. In this confined space, it was difficult not to look at either them or their chunky silver jewelry. Hmongs believe silver keeps their souls weighted down to their bodies. It was somewhat comforting to see all three wearing enough to keep their *inner essence* in place.

In an effort to appear friendly, Bill smiled at the father. His face remained impassive. Bill offered a cookie to the mother. There was no change in her expression either, though she took several.

The chatter of the passengers soon proved more than the man could tolerate. He banged his fist on the top of the truck. Before the startled driver slowed down, he forced his way through our line of knees, grabbed the ladder on the side of the truck, and swung up to sit on the roof with the luggage. A sigh escaped me as the long, curved knife he carried at his waist left our midst.

We were en route to Mae Sai, the notorious border town with Burma. After a bus deposited us there, we joined the tourists swarming through their Sunday morning market. Many were buying "bargain" Burmese gems. Though sold as genuine, they often turned out to be colored glass made in Thailand. When Bill failed to find a Burmese dictionary, he said, "I'm going over to Burma to get one."

"Doesn't that seem a bit foolish? You'll have to get an expensive visa just to cross a bridge to buy one book."

Fortunately, one of the men working at the market promised to bring one back in a couple of hours, so Bill located a restaurant, appropriately called Where Dreams Come, and spent his time eagerly watching for the fellow's return.

While he waited, I visited a jade factory hoping to find a piece of pink jade for my mother, but they only mass-produced small, green Buddha images. On my tour of their factory, I was behind a lady who asked, "Why does the Buddha have such big earlobes?" That was something I had often wondered. She was told, "The heavy jewelry nobility wore stretched their ear lobes."

However, a customer disagreed saying, "No, it was because the nobility began wearing earplugs when they were young. The Buddha's plugs got bigger as he grew and they stretched his lobes."

I still wonder.

We were in the Golden Triangle, the infamous area where Burma, Thailand, and Laos meet, and where much of the world's opium is produced. Bill wanted to stay and learn more. I had no desire to even be there, much less do any exploring.

Since we had been riding in open *songthaews*, fine sand permeated our hair and clothes, even our ears and nose.

"Enough of this grit. I need a swim before we head back to Bangkok!" Bill said.

When he dove into the Mekong I searched for one of the 700-pound shark catfish, hoping he didn't meet up with one. After only ten minutes, he crawled out exhausted. He had barely been able to stay in one place in the swift current.

From here we boarded an air-conditioned bus for Bangkok.

(Bill)

I've met quite a few crazies in my life, but during my month by myself, I met the wildest character in memory. I was staying in the popular Banglapoo backpacker's area, which was convenient for walking to Thammasat. I left the university around five and stopped at the Mango Guesthouse, where I placed my sign in the middle of the table. While I was savoring my beer and people watching, Terry, a six-foot, wiry fellow wearing paratrooper boots and a military camouflage outfit, asked, "What kind of shit you selling?"

I resented his approach but thought it best to explain.

"Nothin's for nothin'," he sneered. "What's your racket?"

"Learning languages and meeting people."

"Where you from?"

"California. But I'm traveling on an Irish passport, and I live in Paris."

"How'd you get the passport?"

"Grandfather was from Cork."

Terry shouted to the waitress, "Bring this asshole Irishman another beer." Then he pulled up a chair.

He was from Ireland. We began talking. I had grown up in a 98-percent Irish neighborhood in Pittsburgh, where my bosom-buddy had the same wild, rebellious look I was seeing now in Terry's eyes. I told him how a bartender had shot my best friend on Christmas Eve after claiming Mick had threatened to throw him through a mirror if he didn't get a free drink.

Terry must have considered this a noble way to go. He patted me on the back like we were buddies. "Just a minute. I want to show you something." He returned, holding a bronze container. "Have a taste," he said.

I took one of the small gray chips.

"Now your body contains a part of my best buddy." Handing me the chalice, he said, "Read this."

I read, "To my dear friend, Charlie. May he rest in peace."

"What are you doing with his ashes?" I asked.

"Taking them to a cave we both enjoyed. I'll blow up the entrance so Charlie can rest in peace."

After some more talk, Terry showed me an official card issued by the Cambodian government. "I'm a bodyguard for the son of Hun Sen, the prime minister. If you ever get to Phnom Penh, ask for me at the Pink Elephant, and I'll show you around."

I figured he was a Walter Mitty commando doing his thing and excused myself to go to the toilet. When I got to the back courtyard, a pockmarked Thai man hollered, "Hold up! You can't go in there. Toilet's broken."

From the way he said it, and because of the other three nail-chewing types with him, I decided it was wise to pee next door. But before I got back to my table, Chicago, a sober friend of Terry's, tapped me on the shoulder.

"It's OK now," he said. "Go ahead."

This time the Thai man nodded his approval, and I went into the toilet that minutes before had been forbidden territory.

When I returned, Terry said, "If you need a gun, I can get you a forty-five."

I answered, "Thanks, but I don't expect to be needing one."

As a police car pulled up, Terry took two passports from his pocket and shoved them in a cubbyhole in the wall behind my chair. "If these thieving bastards start questioning me, give my passports to Chicago."

The cops didn't stop at our table but went to the back, probably for a payoff, though I don't know what transpired.

Then a Cambodian carrying a briefcase and wearing what could have been a Savile Row suit pulled up a chair by Terry. He said he had just arrived from Singapore and whispered something I surmised was the latest news from Phnom Penh. He handed Terry a large manila envelope.

After he left, Terry's wife appeared. She was a well-educated, charming Irish lady who had starred in plays in Dublin and was now taking care of their four-month-old baby girl. Terry's role of commando switched to that of a loving father, as he tenderly rubbed a finger along his baby's cheek.

One doesn't forget a character like Terry.

18

Thailand: Sea Gypsies

(Ina)

Our fall had been rainy, so Bill needed sunshine. After landing in Bangkok, we took an overnight train that bumped and tossed us around on our way to Surat Thani, where we boarded a boat for the island of Ko Samui. Bill had assured me, "Saltwater swims in the Gulf of Thailand might not sound *yuletidy*, but they'll be relaxing."

On arrival Bill checked the port to see if the Chiang Mai prisoner, Jules Beaudet's diving school still existed. It didn't. He then booked us into one of the island's many guesthouses.

Like most of the Westerners in this resort area, we congregated under the open-air, thatched roof at the front of our guesthouse to wait out the short but regular afternoon deluge. Many were young single women who taught English as a second language somewhere in the Far East and were here on vacation. Most men, of whatever age, had Thai girls from Bangkok with them. Floren, a six-foot-four German in his late fifties, said he was with his mother, though we never saw her. Floren was always there and always complaining. "My taxes are too high because the government gives everything to the lazy East Germans," or "They tried to overcharge me at the restaurant last night, but I didn't let them get away with it."

No one wanted to be within his voice range, so we scrambled for a seat away from him. It didn't make much difference. Floren was a lawyer, and he could project his courtroom voice.

During one of Bill's exchange lessons with the cleaning girl, she told him, "That Floren, he come every year looking for a wife, but nobody marry with him. He cheap and have bad breath." A day or so later, she stopped giggling enough to report, "This morning police take him away. He say mother bit bad with bedbugs. No bedbugs here! He say he have to take her to doctor and have to pay there, so no pay hotel bill. But police say, 'You pay, then you go.' We so glad. He one cheap bastard!"

Things were too predictable here. After ten days Bill got restless. "We need a change of scenery. Let's go to Phuket."

I wasn't sure how much of a change another beach would be, but we left. After only a day at their beach, he suggested we visit the sea gypsies. "They tie stones to their waists and use only an air hose, but they can stay more than a hundred feet underwater. And when they're not looking for pearls, they're herding fish into nets."

"There won't be much to see if they're underwater."

Unfazed, he continued, "We can see them dive. Besides, they also gather birds' nests. Some of them will probably be standing on their bamboo ladders, prying the nests off the mountain walls."

"That might be worth a visit," I agreed. Swifts' nests were prized for their aphrodisiac qualities. I couldn't imagine how tiny twigs glued together with bird spit might work, but I was interested in seeing the nests gathered.

I realized soon enough that I should have been more concerned about how we were getting there.

Bill promised to rent the least powerful motorcycle, and to make sure they showed him how everything worked. Bill had never driven one, though I knew well the story of his learning to drive in a forklift on a naval carrier.

"I'll take it slow and easy. We'll have a relaxing tour around the coast," he promised. His less than fifteen-minute instructions didn't qualify him any more than his captain's license had qualified him for our boat trip to Paris. And once again I was foolish enough to climb on, even without a helmet—there was no law requiring them, so none were available.

Driving on the left and ceding to all larger vehicles put us at a disadvantage. Then as we started up the first steep hill, we began to wobble. Bill had trouble shifting gears. After a young girl, who'd likely spent her first months cradled on a motorcycle, came alongside to give instructions, I suggested he pull off the road to do a bit of practicing. He did. In pulling over, he failed to notice the gravel.

One of my legs got scraped when we overturned. After shifting the gears several times, Bill assured me that he now had the hang of it, so I climbed back on.

A large truck swished by sending a gust of wind that pushed us near the sandy edge of the highway. Velocity kept us upright—Bill was closer to full throttle than the "take it easy" he'd promised.

The wind gust of the second truck blew my hat off, forcing me to plant my face firmly in Bill's back.

I didn't see much scenery. If there were sea gypsies around, we couldn't find them. Bill did examine some rickety bamboo ladders that extended hundreds of feet up to the nests.

On the way home, each time Bill throttled up, I squeezed. After we reached the outskirts of town, I waited for the first red light to hop off.

"What are you doing?"

"What does it look like I'm doing? I'm walking back."

As Bill's rental was for two days, our hotel clerk stored the motorcycle for him that night. The next day Bill speculated that I might not want to go with him again.

"Sometimes you are so perceptive!" I said. "And furthermore, I don't intend to ride a motorcycle ever again as long as I live!"

After a grandmother masseuse finessed the tenseness from my muscles—I had never before realized how relaxing having my earlobes massaged could be—I spent a tranquil day reading my guidebook. Even with my library training, I turned down the corner of the page that said: "The season for gathering bird nests runs from

February to July." I then underlined this bit: "Think seriously about whether or not it's worth it to rent a motorcycle on Phuket. The Thais admit that driving on the island is dangerous…A significant number of the people killed are foreign visitors."

Bill returned with a badly bruised shoulder. He got carried away trying to locate one of the birds singing in the rubber plantation, and misjudged his navigation over planks placed across a ditch. He overturned and the motorbike landed on top of him.

Since Bill's shoulder was still giving him trouble, he went back to Paris without his usual Bangkok-by-night stop.

But after this experience, he'll still mention that he plans to take "real lessons" one of these days. And he never fails to say, "Wow, look at that Harley! I'd like to have one of those."

"Why not?" I ask. "A Harley is what Evel Knievel preferred, wasn't it?"

19

Laos: Up the Mekong

(Ina)

After promising this would be the last time he would take me looking for Hill Tribes Bill had us poking around near the Thais-Laos border. It didn't take him long before he said, "Let's go to Laos."

"Why?" I asked.

He looked rather puzzled when he answered, "Because we haven't been there."

The capital, Vientiane, looked interesting, but Bill insisted we go inland. Where and how? Laos had been a monarchy until the Pathet Lao staged their coup in the '70s. This new communist government wouldn't allow packaged tours until '89 and no independent travel until several years later, so there wasn't a plethora of tourist information available.

Ole, the young Dane who asked to go with us said, "Let's go to the Swedish embassy for information."

An official there suggested we visit Luang Prabang. "The paved road ends after fifty kilometers. From there you transfer to an open flatbed truck. The last fifty kilometers take ten hours."

The trip sounded more arduous than ominous until he added, "Two weeks ago Hmong tribesmen ambushed and killed three people on the last part of this mountain road." The CIA had recruited and trained the Hmongs to carry out guerrilla attacks during the Vietnamese War, so whether the motive for this attack had been to embarrass the communist government or was simply banditry seemed irrelevant. Even after we learned that truckers carried automatic rifles and rocket launchers to repel attacks, we stuck to our decision to seek an alternate route.

The thin guidebook I located listed a three-day trip on the Mekong in a triple-decker cargo boat.

"I like that boat idea," Bill said with enthusiasm.

Ole agreed. "Sounds interesting to me. I'd like to go, and I don't want to spend the money to fly."

In the morning a horse-drawn carriage deposited us in front of the only boat in sight. It was neither a triple-decker nor a double-decker. It was a seedy-looking single-decker, but it was the only boat there. A crewmember waved us aboard to what must have been the passenger section, though there wasn't a seat in sight—just bags of salt. Ole and Bill arranged our backpacks on the sacks on what they decided would be the scenic side and left me to guard our choice seats while they went to buy tickets.

"They were a little over three dollars US!" Ole reported, clearly delighted by the money he'd saved.

"They must have charged you the tourist price. And how long will this sack of salt be my resting place?"

They both shrugged.

"It probably depends on the number of stops we make," Bill said, "but I figure the cost is a dollar a day."

"And when do we leave?"

Without looking at me, he gave another indifferent shrug.

Resigned, I settled back to watch three squealing pigs brought aboard, followed by another load of salt. An hour later, when more salt appeared, we were uprooted and moved to another boat that had just docked—another single-decker but a bit larger.

"Do you think we're eligible for this because we're going all the way to Luang Prabang?" Ole asked when he stretched his long legs out on a wooden platform—the only visible upgrade.

Shortly before noon, with the boat fully loaded, we got underway. Ole and Bill had checked out the whole vessel, which included making an acrobatic climb up to the flat roof. An hour later, when I needed directions to the toilet, Bill said, "It's that way, but be very careful."

To go aft I had to bend almost double to navigate between the low ceiling and the salt bags stacked five deep. When I got to the engine room, I could stand up, but there a narrow plank stretching across a yawning pit confronted me. The pit housed the boat's motor. If I happened to slip from the plank when I started across, I'd fall into the whirling fan and lose a limb. If I made it halfway, I'd only land on the hot, oily engine and receive first-degree burns.

My athletic prowess didn't allow me to waltz across like an Olympic gymnast, so I turned sideways with my back to the motor, planted my hands against the ceiling, and moved my left foot several inches, slid my right foot next to it, and shifted my hands. Move…Slide…Shift…Move…Slide. After performing this maneuver about a dozen times, I climbed a couple of steps. *Voilà, la toilette!*

Ducking my head, I entered the enclosure to discover I couldn't stand upright because the roof was too low. But when I tried to sit, there wasn't enough space in front of the toilet to accommodate my knees. I angled my feet into the corners, but that didn't help—there was no way I could pull down my jeans from that position. I had worn jeans and tennis shoes, thinking both would be the perfect attire for this rough-and-tumble river cruise. My present predicament made it evident that a simple little, black evening dress would have been a better choice.

Retreating to the outside, I pulled down my jeans and backed in. With my feet in the doorway, the door wouldn't close, but I held on to the handle swearing not to drink water for the next three days.

A few hours later Ole swung down from the roof, upset about the riverboat gamblers. I knew the trio he was talking about, as Bill had pointed out three seedy-looking individuals when they had come aboard.

"After letting several people win, they cheated all seven of them out of their money," Ole said. "Let me see your dictionary, Bill. I'm going to expose their tricks!"

Ole had graduated from a progressive liberal arts school in Copenhagen, whose program included a heavy dose of philosophy. When he mentioned something about Kant's categorical imperative, Bill cautioned, "Remember where you are. I doubt Western ethics apply anywhere in Laos and certainly not on this boat."

It wasn't long before the three swung down and organized a card game with the six men in our section. Each time Ole spotted their sleight of hand he shook his head. For reasons neither Bill nor I understood, he waited until all but one farmer had lost all his money—this one yanked the purse from his sobbing wife when she wouldn't hand it over. When he lost that, it triggered action. Ole rose to his knees, pointed at the ringleader, and shouted their word for cheater.

His unexpected outburst stunned everyone. The wife swallowed her sobs. The embarrassed husband left for the roof, the other men followed. Laos is a Buddhist country. Peace and harmony may be valued more than confronting the truth. Ole was not only stunned by the silence, he didn't understand the sudden departure of those he was trying to defend.

When one of the gamblers rose to his knees to glare at him, Ole rolled over over onto his stomach and closed his eyes. The gamblers switched their hate-filled looks to us. Now we, too, were the enemy.

About fifteen minutes later, on our approach to the dock we struck a boulder. Our boat shuddered to a halt. Thankfully, their eyes shifted from us to the captain and Rip, the motorman.

We all watched while the two of them waded into the shallow water. Rip loosened the rod holding the rudder. When he brought it up to assess the damage. Bill whispered, "The way that rod is bent, we'll be here a week waiting for a new one."

Rip carried the rod to a boulder. The captain gave it some powerful whacks with a heavy stone and held it up to look it over. Laying it on a flat rock, he whammed it a few more times. Satisfied, they both waded back to the boat and hooked the rod back up to the rudder. The process took less than an hour.

The three of us hung back until all others got off. In the fading light, we maintained our distance from the gamblers. When Ole saw them board another vessel, he said, "They got all they could from our passengers, so now they're taking another boat to do the same thing."

"You should be glad they left," Bill said. "You could have gotten the three of us killed! This boat is no philosophy class. I don't give a shit what your teacher told you about Kant. This is Southeast Asia!"

Ole didn't answer, so things cooled down.

When Bill and I were alone, I suggested maybe he came on a little strong. "Remember, we were youthful idealists once too."

I was thankful most of the original passengers didn't re-board because the three of us created yet another dilemma at bedtime. Our "cruise director" discovered our taller Western frames took up far more room than small Asian bodies, so she relocated several passengers from the wooden platform to give us room to lie down.

I felt guilty over getting special treatment until I realized we hadn't inconvenienced anyone. Salt bags might be lumpy, but they were softer than a wooden floor. With our backpacks for pillows, we stretched out fully clothed.

It's difficult finding a comfortable position if there isn't one.

Rip lit a kerosene lantern and hung it over our heads. I thought it was to preclude any hanky-panky during the night, but Bill assured me it was to keep us afloat. At 3:00 a.m. he was proven right. Rip refilled the lantern and then spent the next hour bailing out water.

I managed a short nap before the captain's radio startled us awake with Laotian rhythms. The music played at full volume while he prepared for first-light departure.

On that second day, I noticed the babies and young children were docile, not solely from lack of sleep. Malnutrition obviously sapped their energy. Bill and I had no appetite seeing five hungry children watch us eat, so we shared our peanut butter and crackers.

When we moored for the night, the men left the boat for a swim. I mentioned virulent liver flukes, but Bill assured me they were only in the south. Rip eyed Bill's blue flippers and asked to borrow them. He performed so many acrobatics for our shipboard entertainment that the sun was low in the sky before the women took their turn in the water. They glided down the gangplank, which ended several feet short of the bank, and waded through the mud in their flip-flops to bathe in a secluded section of the beach. When they came out of the water, they draped themselves with dry sarongs. Though I was invited to join them, my jeans weren't bathing attire. I tied my shoes around my neck, walked the plank in my bare feet, and squished through the mud in search of a toilet.

Bill knew our fellow passengers' language was close to Thai and had been assured that many understood Thai because they'd heard it spoken on TV. He tried a few words but got blank looks. He used words from his dictionary—still no contact. "These farmer dialects have little to do with Laos, much less Thai," he complained. "Forget TV. They must not have radios."

Without any common words, and despite all her horizontal arm waving, we had no clue what problem our cruise director was attempting to resolve on our second night. It turned out to be sleeping arrangements again. Somehow she discovered Ole was not our son, so he couldn't sleep by me as he had done the previous night. And of course I couldn't be next to any male but Bill. After consultations she shooed more people off the platform and assigned us to our new places. Bill, Ole, and I bade each other good night, while Rip again lit the lantern and hung it over our heads.

On the third morning, the boat became noisier when a new passenger put her four chickens, with their feet tied together, on top of a nearby salt sack. I tuned out their squawking when the day's entertainment began—our cruise director was passing around the contents of my makeup kit. The men weren't intrigued with rolling out my lipstick, so she opened Bill's kit. They had great fun clicking the switches of his electric razor and toothbrush. The women began pulling clothes from my backpack and, though it was obvious the garments were too large, tried them on.

How could we object? This was in keeping with the curiosity they displayed each time a new passenger joined the cruise, except the contents of their sacks were immediately inspected and passed around instead of waiting for a get-acquainted period.

We had at last been accepted as part of the group.

20

LAOS: TWO DINNERS AND A BLESSING

(Ina)

I WAS DROWSY until everyone began abandoning our boat the next afternoon. Not knowing what caused the crisis didn't deter us from adding our footprints to the others on the sandy terrain. Having cut my water intake, I bordered on meltdown until Bill pointed toward the wooded hills.

"We're probably moving so fast for fear of a bandit attack," he said.

I rehydrated.

On re-boarding, Ole pointed to the bow of a boat sticking up from the river. "See those six barrels? They're from a boat that sank last week. It's perilously shallow at this bend of the river. Bandits know passengers offload here to allow the boats to pass."

I couldn't imagine how he'd learned this, but I had no doubt every word was true.

At our next stop, we picked up Mama Captain's sister. She spoke French, and from her we learned that calling these people Laotians was a mistake. They refer to both themselves and their country as simply Lao—without an s.

Day three stretched into day four. We navigated around a mother elephant and her baby. We saw several groups of people pan for gold along the riverbank.

Laos is known as the land of a million elephants. A war correspondent had dubbed the country "the land of a million *irrelevants*." I understood his analysis.

Day four finally became day five. With time and a common language, we had developed a friendship with Mama Captain and her sister, and Mama Captain invited us to dinner. I hoped this signaled the last night of our cruise and felt honored to be asked to dine at the captain's table. Again I wished for that little black cocktail dress, but tennis shoes and dirty jeans would have to serve as my formal evening attire.

Mama Captain sent all the other passengers to the roof, commandeering the entire wooden platform for this auspicious occasion. While she cooked on the charcoal brazier she'd set up beside her, Bill opened the wine he'd bought at our last stop and proposed a toast to the captain and his wife for our safe voyage. The second toast was to Rip, the second-in-command, for his multiple talents as savior and entertainer.

As the female guest of honor, I received the first and choice serving. Mama Captain ceremoniously presented me…the head of the chicken.

The speech part of my undergraduate degree hadn't been of much use on this trip, but with all eyes focused on me, I dug deep for any drama tricks I had learned. I knew not to begin eating until my host invited me to do so, and I used this time to breathe deeply and compose myself. An admonition from our guidebook had said "leave a small amount on your plate or the hostess will think she has not provided enough food." I would have no trouble conforming to that bit of etiquette. When invited to begin and to avoid looking at the glassy eye staring up at me, I sliced a tiny piece low on the chicken's neck, as far away from that eye as possible. When I brought it to my mouth, I closed my eyes, feigning unmitigated delight.

My performance must have been sterling—the captain invited us to visit his home the next day.

The floor, the ceiling, the walls, and all the furniture in their two-story home were made of teak. Mama Captain took us to visit their son's primary school, and then we roamed around their village. I felt uncomfortable because the passengers had to wait while we were sightseeing and enjoyable ourselves.

That afternoon we arrived in Luang Prabang and moored against a steep muddy bank. Not wanting to stay on that boat a minute longer, I strapped my backpack in place. As Ole and Bill grabbed an arm, I dug the toes of my tennis shoes into the mud. It took considerable pulling, but the three of us managed my climb up the bank. At last my attire proved itself appropriate.

Bill and I bade Ole an affectionate farewell, and I waited with our packs while Bill went to find us a place to sleep.

"Make sure it has plenty of hot water!" I called after him.

Kon Tip, a lovely young woman who was wearing a beautiful green-and-gold sarong, invited me to sit with her on the porch of her hotel. She told me she had returned from Switzerland to visit her family. "My Swiss boyfriend arranged my escape twelve years ago. As many Lao lived in Northern Thailand, I blended in with the locals, but we had to go to Bangkok to apply for my visa. I didn't look like the Thais in Bangkok, so I hid in a small apartment for the six weeks it took to arrange my papers."

She recommended her hotel so when Bill returned, we checked in. I drank a big glass of water and took a very long, very hot shower.

While eating a pizza in their restaurant, I began reading the literature I had picked up at the desk. I was sharing snippets: "The city got its name after one of its monarchs accepted a Pra Bang, which is a Buddhist statue … Luang means 'great' or 'royal.'" Anxious to begin exploring some of the thirty-two temples the brochure described, I urged Bill, "Eat! Let's go see things!"

When I got no response, I glanced over. One look told me Bill was in no condition to visit anything. Sweat had popped out on his forehead, and he had a sickly pallor.

Over our years together, I had learned Bill rarely reacts like most others. Instead of getting diarrhea, which almost all travelers get, he suffered from a debilitating case of constipation. I also knew my guidebook had categorically stated, "If you require medical attention, we strongly recommend you take a plane to Thailand rather than seek treatment in Laos. There is only one doctor for every five thousand people." I had pointed out that passage when we were first discussing this trip. So what to do now? The word *constipation* wasn't in Bill's *Dictionary of Common Words and Phrases*, and I vetoed his suggestion of saying the word for *no*. Their language has six tones. With my pronunciation, who knew what my *no* might mean?

I reasoned I would need to find a pharmacy, point to the word *diarrhea*, and negate it by shaking my finger.

I located a pharmacy on the main street, and I tried to communicate, but the pharmacist took my elbow and led me outside. He pointed to a row of buildings. When I gave him a questioning look, he pointed again to a specific building. There wasn't a street entrance to what I hoped was a hospital. I followed a woman to the back and entered a pungent-smelling establishment where I made my presentation. I interpreted the gestures to mean, "Bring the patient in."

When I returned, Bill was in less pain, so we retraced my steps. At the hospital he communicated by blocking his rear end with his hand and moving his head in a negative motion.

The doctor laughed. "Oh! *Une* constipation." We all laughed, realizing French was the obvious option.

This was one time Bill didn't have a prolonged conversation. He accepted the medicine; the doctor wouldn't let him pay for his consultation, and we left immediately.

The medicine worked overnight, and the next morning Bill and I visited a Buddhist *wat* (temple) then climbed the rock in the center of town for a view of the mighty Mekong from above.

Their morning market was swarming with Hmongs—possibly the same ones who'd caused us to take the boat rather than the bus.

I couldn't believe they were exchanging their crafted leather and stone artifacts for plastic kitchenware.

In this small city with its leftover French overtones, we savored a baguette as we watched the kids play a circle game—they tried keeping a ball in the air with soccer-style kicks. One of the players had on an artificial leg. We hoped it wasn't caused by one of the two millions tons of bombs dropped on Laos during the Vietnam War to stop traffic along the Ho Chi Minh Tail.

On our last night, we shared a nostalgic dinner with Ole. He was rejoining the boat for his return downstream.

Kon Tip invited us to attend a ceremony to bless the new addition to her home, which she said the Bank of Switzerland had financed. "My family thinks I am the Bank of Switzerland. They never seem to understand I only work there."

The next morning we arrived for the blessing at nine thirty because the monks needed to eat before noon; otherwise they had to go without food until four in the morning.

While Bill sat on a bench out front with the men, Kon Tip's mother took me on a tour of her house. As she was on leave from a Buddhist nunnery, her hair was cropped, though she wasn't wearing her white robe. She showed me her cache of betel nuts along with a pot of lime paste and leaves, conveniently placed beside her rocking chair in the downstairs kitchen. When I showed interest, she invited me to chew some. After seeing the musical South Pacific, I'd always been curious, but I didn't try them. Another missed opportunity!

All fifteen guests congregated in the newly built room the monks had come to bless. The Laos effortlessly folded their legs and settled themselves around the tablecloth spread on the floor. I could roughly simulate their positions, but Bill's legs wouldn't fold right.

When the three monks closed their eyes and began chanting, Kon Tip and her mother left to bring food up from downstairs. The neighbors ignored the monks to converse with each other. Bill squirmed around in an effort to get comfortable. He wasn't always successful keeping his feet off the tablecloth. We were aware that pointing our feet at someone is an insult in Buddhist cultures. The head is holy, but feet are impure. I hoped the monks' eyes were closed tightly and that the others were too busy talking to be offended.

After some thirty minutes of chanting, the senior monk opened one eye to check the time on his pocket watch. He ended the chanting, and we had lunch.

We each had our own bowl of sticky rice. By balling up copious amounts, as they do, I managed quite well with the hot spices we took from the common dishes. I ate their traditional *laap*, made with chopped chicken and eaten with raw vegetables, and I learned how to make my own spring rolls with rice paper. I couldn't identify many dishes, except the fermented fish, but found many of them tasty.

When the monks had to leave, Kon Tip's mother gave each of them one of the woven baskets the women had been making when we arrived. Each now contained a toothbrush and toothpaste, a razor, a packet of blades, soap, and a towel.

As soon as the monks were out the door, their second ceremony began. This was a traditional *baci*, of animist origins. Each guest in turn tied a white cotton thread around Kon Tip's wrist with three knots while wishing her health, prosperity, happiness, and a safe return to Switzerland. Kon Tip said, "The three knots ensure the maximum effect."

They must have thought we needed a safe return too, as Bill had told the men some of our boat experiences. "You risked your lives taking a cargo boat up the Mekong?" one of the men asked him. When they tied the cotton threads on our wrists, they emphasized certain words. I felt sure they were the "safe return" parts.

We gathered up our backpacks, thanked and kissed Kon Tip and her mother good-bye. We left for the airport feeling blessed.

That is, we felt blessed until the man behind the airline counter refused to sell Bill tickets for the one-hour flight back to Vientiane.

"You didn't register when you arrived," he said, "so I can't sell you a ticket

Bill explained that we had come by boat and registered several times along the way.

"How you came doesn't matter. You should have registered when you arrived."

With time running out on our visas, Bill paid the forty-dollar fine.

I was saying my silent good-bye to this delightful city as we awaited takeoff. Bill said, a little too casually, "I'm glad we're both still wearing our sai sin bracelets."

I followed his gaze and began praying that the thirty-two spirits that were guardians of the thirty-two organs in our bodies would extend their magic to our airplane. I so wanted those bald tires to get us back safely.

21

Bali: Beach

(Ina)

After getting so many recommendations from friends to visit Bali, we switched from a Thailand Christmas to an Indonesian one where, instead of cotton balls on Christmas trees, I hoped to see dragons at the Komodo National Park. With luck I might get to visit the World Heritage Buddhist Temple in East Java on New Year's Eve. I was determined to see Bali's many touted attractions during our six-week stay.

Bill wanted beach time, so after a midnight arrival and a few hours' sleep, we went for breakfast in our Kuta Beach hotel's lush garden. While we sat in a covered pavilion overlooking the swimming pool, drinking coffee, and eating mangoes and a banana jaffel, Bill sighed. "What a paradise!"

I agreed.

He rented us a bungalow a short distance from the beach for what the French would say was *trois fois rien*—three times nothing. It included breakfast, hot tea throughout the day, a refrigerator, a bedroom, a sunken living area, and a garden bathroom—a new concept for us. Our bathroom had only three walls. There was a garden where there would normally be a fourth. Beyond the garden was a high wall, ensuring privacy. We found bathing under a full moon does have an effect.

I enjoyed the days and slept well until one night I bolted upright; a rat was crawling over my arm. Bill ran for the two-by-four that secured our front door. He swung but missed.

Assuming the rat had snuck down the wall from our thatched roof, we dragged the bed away from the wall. The next night the rat crawled over Bill's hand. Again Bill missed whacking him. In the morning he went to talk with the manager. "For the last two nights we've had problems with a—"

"A snake!"

"No, a rat."

"Oh, don't worry. Rats won't bother you."

Bill said, "They already have!" and refused to leave until the manager agreed to put some poison on the roof—he tried to talk Bill into letting him fill a box with glue and put it under the bed to trap him, but Bill told him he knew I wouldn't go for that.

But nocturnal visits from a rat, threats of venomous snakes, or heat and humidity didn't dampen our enthusiasm for Bali. Most mornings I sat on our porch, watching the Balinese women begin their day by arranging gifts of food and flowers on high altars to pay tribute to the good gods. They then appeased the evil gods by putting small banana-leaf baskets with incense on doorsteps to keep them from entering the house. The incense burning in these little baskets were to entice the evil spirits down to earth—assuring them that they too were being honored. As evil spirits only travel in straight lines, baskets were also placed at intersections.

Each afternoon Bill headed for the beach, where he spread his language sheet in front of two ancient Hindu statues that hid the toilets. They provided him with shade, and most people made their ways to the toilets sometime during the day.

The Balinese consider their language sacred. They don't use it with foreigners so Bill exchanged English and French for Bahasa Indonesian. He became such an attraction that an article about his exchange appeared in the *Kanya Bakti*, the major English-language newspaper in Indonesia.

Two of Bill's students were Christians—a rarity. Indonesia is the most populous Muslim country, and except for the Balinese, almost everyone is Muslim. Eager for Christian boyfriends, the students asked for Bill's help in finding them. He undertook the challenge but admitted defeat after three days. Men didn't come to Bali looking for religious girls.

At six o'clock, when things cooled down, I joined Bill to watch the often-photographed sunset and talk with his new friends. From Merry, who sold sarongs, I learned that most Balinese street and beach vendors didn't live in Kuta, but returned to their home villages after their day's work. They spent much of their time preparing for one of their celebrations. With sixty major festivals and six rites of passage for each person in the village, they were kept busy.

There were a dozen or more corn-on-the-cob carts, but we bought from the boy who called himself "The Dancing Girl." He executed graceful pirouettes while he spread our steamed corn with butter and hot sauce before grilling it over his charcoal fire. On his stand were two pictures of his drag performances at a local bar.

While munching our corn, we strolled near the water, where hawkers weren't allowed. We wanted to be spared the constant "Wanna buy a watch?" from boys who seemed to be everywhere flipping open a box strapped to their necks to show off their collections of "designer" watches available at "very good prices." On the inside covers, they had printed their business names, which might be Edy, Fread, or Bobb.

On our stroll back into town, someone would invariably ask, "Where are you going?" We realized this had to be a greeting, as complete strangers wouldn't be interested in our destination. Merry told us the appropriate answer was, "Walking, walking." If they stopped to talk, I claimed three sons. Not having a son is bad. Some believe any childless woman will suckle a giant caterpillar in her next life.

After our walk came our most taxing daily decision: which restaurant should we choose? Restaurants of every kind were there, and they were good. They also had the inevitable McDonald's and KFC, which we didn't try. The latter served rice—a must for Asians. They mixed it with their French fries, and used the chicken skin as a wrap.

I refused to go back to one restaurant after Bill asked for something and the waitress turned red and went to the kitchen and didn't come back. Another waitress had to serve us.

Bill told me he had made rapid progress with the language because verbs have no conjugation and repeating a word forms its plural. Clearly his pronunciation had not progressed as well. A Balinese friend told him his pronunciation of "Do you have chopsticks?" translated as, "Do you have a tight pussy?"

I pried him away from his language lessons to accompany me on a temple tour. Unfortunately, its attraction was the temple's Monkey Forest. One man didn't heed our guide's warning about their thievery so he lost his glasses. For much of our time there the guide poked at the monkey thief with a long pole—without success.

I did learn that menstruating women aren't allowed to prepare temple food or to attend temple celebrations. Their blood is considered so potent that if it ever touches a man's scalp, he will become impotent and follow his wife around like a dog. But hungry evil spirits enjoy male blood, especially if it's spilled at one of their highly ritualized cockfights.

I wasn't disappointed that we'd missed these often-scheduled events.

Of course, Bill wanted to visit a prison. I declined his invitation. Good idea, for when he returned he told me: "I walked a mile, got drenched in a downpour, and chased by a vicious dog. Then the guard said, 'You need official authorization.'

"As I turned to leave, a sleek, black limousine pulled up. The guard greeted the Chinese driver with a bow. When he went in I spoke to this VIP's female companion with kindergarten Chinese.

"'I speak English,' she said and handed me a card with the address of their art gallery in Ubud, and another for their massage parlor in Kuta.

"When her partner returned, he handed the guard the equivalent of ten dollars in *rupiah*. After the guard saw her wave goodbye, he became friendly. 'My name is Wyan. Where are you staying?'

"I told him, Kuta Puri Bungalows.

"'I've finished work, and I'm on my way there. Would you like a ride?'

"Wyan rolled his motorbike out and I hopped on the back. On the way I asked, 'Was that fellow a friend of the director of the prison?'

"'No, he served a year here for tax evasion.'

"Then why does he come back?

"'If you're rich and Chinese, and you want to stay healthy in a Bali prison, you pay.'

"I wasn't surprised when he pulled into the tourist office belonging to his brother. On the back of one of his brother's business cards, he wrote the name Helmut Schmidt and handed it to me.

"'If you come to the prison tomorrow, ask for him.'

"Is it OK to bring my wife?

"'Sure, but leave a couple dollars inside your passport.' As he left he said, 'Remember my brother can take you anywhere on the island, and he'll give you the lowest price.'"

The next day I agreed to visit the prison if we took a taxi. We took batteries, chocolates, figs and dates. Helmut appeared puzzled by our presence until Bill explained he thought he might want an outside contact.

Unlike in Thailand these prisoners had freedom to walk around and visit with each other during the daylight hours, so Helmut showed us around the courtyard.

"It's not bad here if you behave," he said. "But being in the hole is rough. I've been there several times because when I make booze, I get drunk and fight."

His Japanese wife and five-year-old son lived in an adjoining section. He was incarcerated for heroin smuggling and was given a long sentence, but was scheduled for early release. He didn't tell us how much his mother had paid or who she had paid to get him out.

With the must-visit prison tour over, I didn't think I could get Bill away from his language exchange again until I found this brochure in a tourist office. I felt sure he wouldn't resist this.

> Drive up to Kedisan Village, from where we will sail by private baot to Trunyan Village. For about forty five minutes sailing from Kedisan to Trunyan village where the destination of sight seeing is Trunyan village in an isolated village where is located between on the lake shore and the mountainous area. Fishing and agricultural activities are the people life. That village is really very famous in the world due to its different culture among Balinese. The strangeness is the corpse is not buried, but lied down on the grave yard under the big tree without smelling. Only by boat we can reach the cemetery. Let's see while in Bali.

Bill was intrigued, even eager to go, but our visas expired before the next cremation took place.

"Don't give up hope. This won't be our last chance," Bill said. "Let's come back here next year!"

22

CAMBODIA: SMOKING THE COBRA

(Bill)

I'd heard so much about Cambodia's being the Wild East that instead of going to Bangkok for my usual extra month, I decided to take a look at Cambodia. Ever since reading about Angkor Wat in Richard Halliburton's *Book of Marvels* in the eighth grade, I had dreamed of going there.

It fulfilled all my expectations.

After seeing it, I caught a flight on Royal Cambodian Air to Phnom Penh, where I booked into the Sunshine Hotel. The porter who carried my suitcase spoke English, so I asked if he would make me a sign in Khmer and wrote my language-exchange message on a piece of notebook paper. I gave him a black Magic Marker and a manila folder. Within a half hour, he proudly handed me my folder with the message neatly printed in English.

"That's very nice," I said, trying not to look surprised. "Now could you write the same thing in Khmer on the other side?"

This miscommunication proved helpful. When the expats or tourists here asked me what I was doing, I simply showed them the other side.

My guidebook listed the Foreign Correspondence Club as a good starting place for a first night in Phnom Penh, so I climbed a flight of stairs and entered a prosperous English pub. Most of the tables were occupied, including all those with views of the Tonle Sap River. Two Westerners sat at the far end of the bar. I sat near the middle, one stool away from another Westerner, and ordered a mug of Angkor beer.

The Cambodian bartender asked, "How long you been here?"

"Less than twenty-four hours."

"First time?"

"Yeah."

I was interested in finding out about Terry, the unforgettable guy I met in Bangkok. I had asked the hard cores on Soi 13 if they knew him. Several did. My former nemesis, Ray, had said, "Yeah, Terry was a bodyguard in London until he got in trouble with the law."

"Do you happen to know a bar called the Pink Elephant?"

"Sure," he said. "It's just a block and a half down this street."

He left, but I gathered from the friendly nod from the guy on my right that he was open to conversation. So I said, "I hear this is a wild city."

"Can be. It's OK as long as you're careful."

"You work here?"

"Been here almost two years. I'm a photographer."

"Maybe you've heard of a guy named Terry."

"Sure, I know him."

I moved my beer and sat next to him. "I met him in Bangkok a couple of years ago. Is he still a bodyguard for Hun Sen's son?"

"Now he's trains his bodyguards."

"Hun Sen a good prime minister?"

"He's a wily, one-eyed Machiavellian who knows when and how to get rid of his opposition."

"Does he get along with King Sihanouk?"

"They're both shrewd and switch direction like wind vanes."

He ordered another beer and continued. "Hun Sen was a Khmer Rouge officer who defected to Vietnam in '77. As for King Sihanouk, he went along with the French, the Khmer Rouge, and the others who controlled the political scene. In between he directed and starred in nine movies."

"Does he hold the power?"

"As long as he doesn't alienate the military Hun Sen will let him play his part."

"Thanks for the information. I'm going for a look at the Pink Elephant."

"Enjoy yourself, but be careful."

I found the place and ordered a beer. "Do you know a guy named Terry?" I asked the bartender.

He laughed. "Most everybody does." He handed me a copy of the *Bayon Pearnik*, a tourist magazine. He pointed to an article—"Smoking the Cobra. "The character in that story called Gorilla is Terry."

I read, "Gorilla has a deserved reputation for instigating full-blown insanity. He can send those around him running for cover like a live grenade."

This was the gist of the article:

> Gorilla asked Harry Palms, "You wanna drink some cobra blood on New Year's Eve?"
>
> Harry knew the evening would prove exciting so he said, "Sure."
>
> New Year's Eve, Gorilla appeared for the Blood Party dressed in black—pants, shirt, boots and woolen knit hat pulled close to one brow—the ruthless Southeast Asia pirate look…His beard was a long black pigtail that hung from his chin. They headed for a restaurant on Monivong Boulevard.
>
> After a price was negotiated, the cobra was delivered in a blue fish net…Gorilla volunteered to kill it himself and reached into the bag and pulled out the

angry four-foot reptile. The cobra's mouth hadn't been tied correctly…It whipped from Gorilla's grip and locked its fangs into the seam of his black Levis. Gorilla was skinny, so the seam saved him from spending the night in the Calmette morgue.

The sight of a loose cobra sent the customers running and chairs, dishes, and glasses crashing to the floor. Two customers stopped at the door and shouted, "*Barang lop lop! Barang lop lop!*" (Crazy foreigner! Crazy foreigner!)

Gorilla trapped the cobra with his boot and cut off his head. He laid the severed head on the table, then lifted the serpent above his glass of Khmer whiskey and squeezed in some blood. He took a few sips, closed his eyes, and paused a moment. "This blood is bullshit. Let's smoke the venom."

Gorilla sliced open the venom glands and spread a healthy coat of poison on a cigarette. He took several deep inhales. Then he leaned back in his chair and, with a somewhere else look in his eyes, gave sighs of pleasure as he stroked his pigtail beard.

Onlookers waited for him to fall off his chair—they knew cobra venom could lead to paralysis or death.

Gorilla sat back and murmured, "Now this is the real thing."

After reading the article, I asked if Terry came to the Pink Elephant.

"Yes, but not so often since the British owner died of a heart attack. You can usually find him now around the corner, in the Rising Sun Bar."

The next evening I visited the Rising Sun and recognized Terry sitting with five others at one of the outside tables. I couldn't miss him, not with his pigtail beard.

I went to the bar and ordered a beer. Terry had been half blasted the afternoon I met him in Bangkok. A few years had passed, so I doubted he would recognize me without my sign. I tuned in to the conversation of two English guys sitting two stools away: "Yeah, if a Cambodian pulls a gun on you, you'd better let him take whatever you got."

"He did. He handed him his wallet but then jumped him when he turned to get on his motorcycle. I hear the guy will never walk again."

As they were talking, Terry walked past. He returned from the WC, laid one hand on my shoulder, and asked, "Where have I seen you before?"

"Mango Guest House in Bangkok."

"I remember now. You're that fake Irishman."

"And you're the one who serves human chips. Did you blow up your cave?"

"No, Charlie loved the Mekong, so I decided he'd prefer to flow with it. When I lowered the chalice, the damn thing wouldn't sink. It must have twirled around for three minutes. I had to push Charlie under with the paddle. Come have a drink with us."

After introductions, Bob, one of Terry's friends and an American Vietnam vet, was preparing to leave. "What brings you here?" he asked me.

"I'm a traveler," I replied.

"I was too. Came for three months. Been here nine years."

Before revving up his powerful cycle, he hollered to the group, "Don't forget to show up at the airport tomorrow."

Terry explained a ceremony would be held to honor and return bodies of Americans killed in a helicopter rescue attempt.

Before I left, Terry said, "Once a month about twenty of us charter a boat for an all-night beer bash on the Mekong. It's always on a Friday. The next one will be in ten days. You're invited."

23

Cambodia: Living on the Edge

(Bill)

I HAD NO intention of going on a river trip with those wild men. I could end up getting thrown in the river. I did, however, want to find out more about Phnom Penh, so I went back to the sidewalk café at the Pink Elephant, since their terrace attracted many expats.

Paul, a very stable Brit I met there, had no use for Terry. He made artificial limbs—something needed in this long-suffering country. He told me about Terry's remark. "'You make 'em, I break 'em.' That bastard would make fun of anything," he said.

Later I visited another establishment with an Australian name: the Walkabout. It never closed. Patrons spent their days on barstools or at the pool table. Those who had been carousing elsewhere came here when elsewhere closed. A few recovered with plates of sausages, eggs, hash browns, and baked beans; others never sobered up.

It was about ten in the evening. There were customers at the U-shaped bar, three playing pool and eight sitting at tables. I sat down and put my language sign on the bar. Not a soul paid any attention. All eyes focused on a husky, six-foot Aussie in his late twenties, whose long, blond curls hung to the shoulders of his bright-orange shirt. He was patting around on accompanied girls, hanging his ass over the pool table, and taking sips from others' drinks. A sober-looking American sitting next to me said, "If that asshole bothers me, it won't last more than a minute."

Before I could comment, a middle-aged guy in a blue business suit greeted my neighbor. The newcomer said he'd been reporting to parliament all week. My neighbor then asked him for legal advice. His reply concerned intricacies of Cambodian law beyond my comprehension.

The lawyer glanced at his watch and said, "Sorry I can't stay for a drink, but give me a call if that doesn't work out. I know both your next-door neighbors are cabinet ministers, so you shouldn't have any trouble getting it through."

When his friend left, I said, "I couldn't help hearing snatches of that conversation, much of which was code to me."

"Me too. He's the best lawyer in Cambodia. Used to be a partner at a big law firm in California."

"Why would he change that for Phnom Penh?"

"Few people can explain the attraction of this place, me included."

"Are you a lawyer?"

"No, I'm an engineer. I work for the UN drilling wells, but I have other business here too."

I learned he had worked in areas controlled by the Khmer Rouge.

"They tolerated my presence," he said. "But one day they decided the village chief was defying them, so I was told it would be wise to get out of town for a couple of days. I did. When I returned, the chief's mangled body was hanging from a tree."

"I don't think I'd want your job."

"It gets me nervous, but I used to be a Navy SEAL. That training prepared me for dangerous situations."

The Long Haired Aussie came over to talk to two of his friends. When he left to go to the restroom, my neighbor told them, "If I were you, I'd tell him to take it easy. It's dangerous acting the way he is in Phnom Penh."

They didn't appear to appreciate the advice. However, one went to the restroom and the Aussie came out. "I understand you don't like me," he said to the engineer.

"I think you're acting like an ass," he answered.

The Aussie grabbed his arm. "Fuck off," he said, giving him a shove.

The SEAL grabbed him under the armpits, raised him off his feet, and threw him headfirst into a telephone hanging on the wall.

The Aussie jumped up and pulled back a fist. Before he could swing, the SEAL grabbed his belt and shoulder and whammed his head against the wall. His head bled. One of his buddies tried to stop it with a handkerchief. The others helped him to a cab and headed for a hospital.

I said, "I timed you—forty seconds."

"My adrenaline was flowing. That bastard gave me no choice."

I left the Walkabout knowing why Dave, my friend in Bangkok, had said: "Don't take your wife to Phnom Penh. Fly her in to see Angkor and then get the hell out of there."

With my curiosity satisfied about the Wild East scene, I wanted to see some of the sights. Each time I left my hotel the young motorcyclists competed to be my guide.

"Want to go to the range?" one asked.

"What's that?"

"Place you can fire a Kalashnikov, or an M-21, or most any other gun you want."

I didn't want.

"What about Kilometer 11?" another asked.

"What's there?"

"Girls…some as young as eleven. You don't have to take any. You can just go look."

"No, thanks."

The Royal Palace and the Silver Pagoda were not high on the list of attractions they were accustomed to taking their clients to see.

"Then what about the Killing Fields?" another asked.

When I decided to visit them, they flipped a coin to see who would take me.

Before we roared off, the others shouted, "Me! Tomorrow! Me...Take me tomorrow!"

We zigzagged around chickens, hogs, and the usual deep holes on a washboard dirt road during the fifteen-kilometer ride.

I paid my two dollars to enter what had previously been a loganberry orchard. Now it contained the remains of more than sixteen thousand men, women, and children the Khmer Rouge had massacred between 1975 and 1978. Pol Pot, the communist revolutionary leader, had been the guiding force behind this murderous regime. His goal was to change Cambodia into a Maoist, peasant-dominated cooperative society. He'd picked up his Maoist ideas while studying in Paris. Ironically he'd received some of his early education in a Buddhist wat.

Arrows pointed to paths leading to the communal graves—a hundred and fifty had been excavated—forty-five were open for viewing.

What an eerie feeling to see human bones exposed. Some of the victims had been blindfolded and clubbed or hacked to death to save bullets. In the third pit, blue bits of clothing still stuck to the bones.

At the fifth grave, the last I visited, I passed a Buddhist monk escorting an elderly woman. She held a handkerchief to her eyes, wiping tears. I saw only one other visitor, a stoop-shouldered old man leaning on a black umbrella. He remained motionless, staring into one of the trenches for as long as I watched him.

A *stupa*—a Buddhist shrine—had been erected in the center of the orchard. Eight thousand skulls exhumed from the mass graves lay stacked behind its clear glass walls.

The orchard was calm. The birdcalls somehow added to the macabre atmosphere.

I left, depleted.

The next day, not wanting more tragedy, I told the motorcycle guides I was going across the street. I figured the most pleasant place to learn a little Khmer would be on one of the stone benches bordering the Tonlé Sap River.

My first customer was a gray-haired man in his sixties who wanted to speak French. Cambodia became a French protectorate in 1863. When Paris fell in 1944, the Japanese expelled the French, but after World War II Cambodia became an autonomous state within the French Union. But in '53 King Sihanouk dissolved the parliament and declared Cambodia's independence.

Considering this history, I had anticipated many people would know French. Few did, and those not yet fifty wanted to speak or learn English.

The wide boulevards and much of the architecture, though crumbling, were French. The Cambodians had adopted one custom that thankfully had been abandoned in Paris: the moment an innocent ventured onto the grass, a guard blew his whistle, accompanied by vigorous finger pointing. The patchy grass area along the walk bordering the river is held in higher regard than the French language.

My gray-haired companion came five times and helped me write a phonetic thirty-five-word story. Khmer has the largest alphabet in the world—seventy-four letters, and the pronunciation is difficult. My phonetics was so bad my story could not be understood. The listener had to make so many corrections; he soon gave up. I, too, have given up on all Khmer.

I eventually visited the infamous former Khmer Rouge prison S21, now the Tuol Seng Genocide Museum. Though the vast majority of prisoners had been Cambodians, the victims also included ten other nationalities—anyone accused of opposition to Pol Pot. They had been shackled to the damp cement floor and left to shiver through long nights without mats or blankets.

The guards had been more terrifying than the lack of doctors or medicine. At age ten to fifteen, both males and females had begun training for this job. These teenagers often proved more sadistic than their adult counterparts.

Ten regulations were posted in each cell. Three of them stuck with me:

> While getting lashes or electrification, you must not cry at all.
> Do nothing. Sit still and wait for my orders. If there is no order, keep quiet.
> If you do not follow all the above rules, you shall get many lashes with electric wire.

The pictures of prisoners hanging on the cell walls showed their fear and horror. For two days after my visit, I had flashbacks, visualizing the photos of prisoner 114 and prisoner 870—two teenage girls who must have been sisters. They had the most frightened expressions.

24

BALI: LAND OF THE MONSOONS

(Ina)

THIS CHRISTMAS, EVEN thinking we might travel around Bali was delusional. Bill had arrived in Kuta with two goals in mind. The plume on his Irish coat of arms began to wave in Paris, so he came to Bali to continue writing his childhood adventures. But more of a priority was the reconstruction of his two language books our taxi driver had driven off with when we left Bali the year before. Bill's briefcase had contained cash, credit cards, his electric razor, and who knows what else. He mourned only the loss of his two books.

Our garden-bathroom bungalows were closed for renovations, so Bill rented us an air-conditioned room at Fat Yogi's—it's lauded for its Australian charcoal grilled steaks. In my effort to cope with my two disappointments, I pretended to be the actress, Esther Williams, swimming among orchids in their pool. They were really frangipani that fell from two overhanging trees, but they were as pretty as orchids and had a lovely aroma—a better resemblance to orchids than I was to Esther.

Bill set off to the Matahari Department Store to buy what he deemed the best and cheapest selection of multilingual books he'd ever come across. He had packed the leftover pieces of his leather jacket, so now both his reconstructed books would be black-leather bound. Before major construction began, he posted signs on the inside front covers offering a $300 reward for their return—no questions asked. How disparate were our value systems! I failed to understand why he thought his homemade books were worth anywhere near that if they contained info like this:

>Favorite Words
>Brain—ubongo—Swahili
>Handkerchief—hankachi—Japanese
>Sleep—la la—Swahili.
>Words That Sound Like or Describe Their Meanings
>Womb—moder liv—Swahili
>Adulterer—dillay—Hindi
>Grape—vin' bero—Esperanto
>Wordiest (Swahili)
>Cherry—mamna ya tunda dogo
>Beef steak—kipande cha nyama ya ng'ombe

But years ago I realized I didn't have to understand Bill to be grateful he was in my life, as he kept it interesting.

My job, as in Paris, was to read what he'd written and make suggestions. But the rasping noise he made while ripping off long sections of Scotch tape for his book construction far exceeded my tolerance level. We moved to a nearby bungalow with more space.

There, each morning, a young man delivered our breakfast. After placing the tray on our porch, Gusti bowed to bless first our house and then us. His name interested me. I had been curious about names, and learned they, rather than occupations, identified the castes in Bali—though a person's caste doesn't have much importance here. The Balinese are free to pursue any occupation they wish unless they belong to the high priest caste. But everyone has one of four names in their four castes. Every first child—regardless of whether a boy or a girl—is named Wayan. The next one is Nyoman. Then Made (two syllables). The fourth, Ketut. If more children are born, the names are repeated. Since ninety percent of the Balinese belong to the lowest caste, these names get quite a workout.

I made frequent visits to Tulip's Beauty Shop for body therapy, as she called her massages. Tulip is the professional name she has chosen. She said most people who worked used names of their choosing rather than their real names. From her I learned that Gusti belonged to the Wesia, the third warrior caste. This meant other Balinese spoke to him in middle rather than low Balinese.

Tulip or her assistant either carried or pulled her baby around on a modified version of a roller skate. Balinese babies are considered little gods and aren't allowed to crawl, as crawling is considered a barbaric act of animals. One of their six rites of passage takes place 105 days after birth. Only after this rite is an infant allowed to make contact with the impure earth.

Each morning, before it got hot and steamy, I did my fruit shopping, which included salak, a crisp, not-very-sweet apple-size fruit known as "snake fruit" since its outside resembled the brownish scales of a reptile. The morning after I learned durians were in season, I made an effort to find them. I knew they were big, expensive, and malodorous, because the friend who had recommended we visit Bali told me of their often-posted sign: "No smelly fruits allowed here." He said, "The first time I saw it, I turned to my partner and quipped, 'Do you think they mean us?'"

I was on the verge of buying one when a woman standing next to me advised against the purchase.

"They're an acquired taste," she explained.

As I was still curious, I ordered a slice at a restaurant. I realized how right she was—a moldy Gorgonzola would have tasted better.

One morning some hand woven baskets appeared in our pool area, and the manager informed me that a celebration to bless the property would take place the following day. Afraid that we might interfere, I asked, "Would you prefer we not swim at that time?"

"No problem," he assured me.

Nevertheless we stayed at the far end of the pool; but if we hadn't, we wouldn't have disturbed anyone. The priest set up his table poolside. He was intent on his chanting; the people attending weren't. They chatted rather noisily as they drank tea and ate fruit from the baskets. But when he rang his bell, they rushed to sit quietly on the edge of the pool until he sprinkled them with holy water.

So our second year in Bali, I returned home blessed but still untraveled. Bill came with me as he had more writing to do.

25

BALI: A TRANSFORMED KUTA BEACH

(Ina)

ON OUR THIRD Christmas we found Kuta Beach transformed. The first evening we walked there to get corn on the cob from The Dancing Girl, we couldn't find him. Instead of a dozen carts, now there were two. And where were the open-air bars vacationers sat drinking their Bintang beer? Merry was no longer selling sarongs, as without beer there were few vacationers on the beach. Bill learned that a law the city council passed forbade bars on the beach. This had caused their unemployment to rise. This became more apparent the evening I went for a walk by myself. I was stopped and asked, "Are you looking for a boy? I'm a nice Indonesian boy."

The second big change was the weather. Though December was the rainy season, we had experienced an occasional short downpour on our two previous visits. This year showers became daily occurrences, so we bought umbrellas. When the heavy rains lasted more than an hour, we upgraded to rain capes. The sewers couldn't handle the runoff, so we walked around the puddles. Each day they got deeper and wider, and instead of walking around them, we wore flip-flops and began wading through them.

"Transport?" was a question always asked when we were out *walking, walking*. This meant a taxi, a motorcycle, or a *bemo*—a small truck with seats in the back. Now young men would come up, bend over, and ask if I wanted transport on their backs through the deep water.

Rain didn't interfere with Bill's writing, but one evening on our way to eat I slipped on moss on the water-covered sidewalk, so we moved to another location. Not long after, we found a thin covering of water on our bathroom floor.

I didn't want another encounter with the manager. The first time I had reported a leak in a pipe and said our bathroom floor was wet, he sounded puzzled and asked, "What do you want me to do about it?"

"Fix it," I had answered, somewhat mystified that he wouldn't realize what seemed obvious to me. I hadn't understood this cultural difference. When the Balinese take their baths, they throw containers of water over themselves. For them a wet floor is the norm.

My second *faux pas* had been mentioning how amusing I found the intermittent hiccupping sounds the geckos made during the heavy rains. He was very polite while informing me that these sounds had religious significance. He didn't explain, and I was too embarrassed to ask questions.

The water standing on the bathroom floor wasn't the result of a sluggish drain, as we'd supposed. That night, after another steady downpour, the water in the yard in front of our bungalow rose above our porch and seeped under our front door. We woke to find several items bobbing around our bed.

After six weeks of rain, I was ready to leave. Bill wanted to stay two more weeks before going to Bangkok. I opted to go back to the boat and do some much-needed work in our garden. Paris weather might not be great in winter, but it was better than this.

(Bill)

It was like old home week when I arrived at Soi 13. Ray, the Aussie, was civil—civil for Ray, that is. On my first night, I spoke with an Ethiopian, a Dane, about ten female Thais, and a young guy who had fled the Sudan.

Later, I visited the Ther Mae Tea Room. At the bottom of the stairs, I turned left and headed for the table of the two Chinese owners. Never had I seen so much booze sold so fast. My Singha beer arrived before the Chinese bartender scribbled the order and punched the slip on the spike in front of him.

The Ther Mae's basement was almost the size of a football field. The oval bar in the middle resembled a running track. A jukebox on the left attracted two or three brave couples attempting to dance, but the place was too crowded. The booths that lined this left side were packed with men and freelance girls negotiating possibilities for the evening.

I observed the interactions until the smoke got to me. With my beer in hand, I fought my way through the pack of men and girls to stand near the police-bouncer who stood in a corner by an exit door where fresh air came in. Five more minutes of the smoke was all I could take. I retreated up the stairs and into the hotel lobby where a leather chair faced the restroom. A cluster of girls waited to primp at the two mirrors. Two girls, at these key places, combed, powdered, and renewed mascara until they were elbowed out. Before leaving they pulled down the top of their dress to show more cleavage.

Two stalls separated the basins from the three urinals. The competition for these thrones was greater than for the mirrors.

Mama Pee Pee, who was more than a bit loony, ruled the toilet. When she wasn't busy distributing towels or selling condoms and mint candies, she was doing the hula and waving her arms along with her favorite Thai music. When the spirit moved her, she grabbed the shoulders of one of the men at the urinals and shook him while he peed. Then, turning him around, she pointed to his penis. By spreading her palms, she mimed it a foot long, and gave the fellow a thumbs-up and a pat on the back.

I considered the Ther Mae Tearoom a weird mix. Sad. Unique. Entertaining.

26

France: A River, a Taste of Mustard, and Wine

(Ina)

France wanted no part of our motto, "Neither rain nor snow nor heat nor gloom of night..." When the Seine went on a rampage and flooded the gravel path in front of our boat, they suspended mail delivery. As the Seine rose, so did our boat, forcing the gangway to slant downward until half of it was submerged. The city delivered sawhorses and planks so Bill was able to extend it. We could then walk to the Bureau de Poste.

When spring came and my daffodils bloomed, I corralled those that had washed downstream and replanted them, but when I discovered my mammoth Texas sunflowers had somehow made it two hundred yards upstream I told Bill, "If the Seine can force my sunflowers to bloom in *her* yard, I think we should investigate to see where she gets such power."

As Bill enjoys driving through wine country and the Seine's source is in Burgundy, he was ready.

"Since we're going that way, why don't we try wine corking as Michel does? We won't get much. Just enough to learn how it's done."

He agreed and I visited the two wine recycling bins in our area. Although they're emptied regularly, these two containers frequently overflow, so I collected bottles quickly.

The Seine gets her name from a Celtic word meaning "similar to a snake." She makes eight large right hand loops between our boat and the English Channel. We had been that way often. Downstream, at Rouen—where Jeanne d'Arc was burned at the stake and her ashes were scattered in the Seine—we saw the tall sailing ships that would rendezvous there from various ports around the world. And we had seen her empty into the English Channel, but we had never followed her the other way.

The afternoon we started, Bill first made a stop for a sentimental look at the *Wanderer*. With my still-vivid memories, I wasn't eager for a revisit, and Bill was upset when he found she had undergone a name change. "*Fudo* is a dog's name," he complained. Her butterfly wings had been removed. The green-and-white paint had been changed to orange-brown, and the magnificent oak mast had been taken down. When he saw the anchor and parts of the hull rusting, we left.

We then drove past the Île de la Cité where Paris began more than two thousand years ago as a Celtic fishing village called Lutetia. In a half hour, we pulled up along the bank of the Marne.

When we taught in Paris we sometimes drove to this largest branch of the Seine to watch the Gypsy kids rolling tires and wrestling their dogs or one another.

"It hasn't changed much," Bill said, pointing to the woman who was picking up a baby crawling around in the dirt. She settled the baby astride her hip for her trip into Paris to beg.

At Fontainebleau, Bill said, "Let's spend the night in Sisley's home town."

"Great idea!" This Impressionist painted our local café-tabac in 1897, the year of The Great Flood when the Seine turned the streets in front of our boat into a canal.

Bill parked in the lot by the Loing River and we walked by Sisley's house. The sound of the old water mill here lulled us to sleep that night.

In the morning Bill said, "Let's skip Montereau. It's just an industrial town."

"But another river joins the Seine there, doesn't it?"

"It's the Yvonne, but there's nothing there."

We zoomed through the area and Bill didn't slow down until we got to the valley where the Aube joined the Seine. Flowering trees grew along the banks, and we stopped for a picnic and a long walk.

"This road doesn't continue along the river, so let's go to where Vercingétorix surrendered to Julius Caesar," Bill said.

"What's the connection?"

His rationale: "It's quite simple. Vercingétorix was the national hero of Gaul. M. Russis was our Greek hero. While he was dredging the Seine he found a sword from the time of the Gauls, so he had a connection with Vercingétorix. M Russis gave us his mooring, so we will be paying tribute to both him and the Seine."

I concurred with his so-eloquently-convoluted reasoning.

Bill spent time there peering over the rope barrier bordering an archeological dig, perhaps dreaming of discovering the edge of a sword sticking out of a trench. And from the top of this steep hill, we looked down on Alesia, where Caesar and his Roman legions lay siege and starved the Celts into submission, thus making Gaul part of the Roman Empire.

Our destination was nearby and I was excited when we arrived. We parked and followed a well-trodden path.

"There's the grotto!" Bill said, "Look at the goddess Sequana. She's sitting on her boat."

"That's it? That dribble is the source? I expected a waterfall or at least gushing water."

"Then come look! Over here she becomes a trickle."

What a disappointment! It was hard to believe my sunflower migration originated with a Celtic goddess, sitting in a boat that had grounded on a dribble.

"Mission accomplished!" Bill said, "on to the wine!"

In nearby Dijon we bought several jars of mustard, and after dining on boeuf bourguignon, a specialty of the area, we stopped for the night in a terraced vineyard on the other side of town.

By midmorning, in Nuits-Saint-Georges, we located the cave Michel recommended and began tasting. We both liked the Pinot Noir.

"I think we'd better sample the others since we'll be drinking whatever we pick for several months," Bill said.

Though we stuck with the Pinot he told the proprietor, "We'll take a cask of this Chablis too."

With our forty liters, Bill chose the quickest route back to Paris, and the next morning, as the corks soaked in hot water, he put the cask of Chablis on the sink board. I filled a bottle and handed it to him. He fitted the cork in the brass corker Michel had loaned him, positioned it, and pushed down. We had corked our first bottle!

Our production line was in full gear when Michel stopped by on his inspection tour. I handed him a glass. He first studied the wine by swishing it around to observe the color. He took a sip and held it in his mouth for a moment before swallowing, as any Frenchman would do. He pronounced it "quite acceptable," but he pursed his lips when he saw our bottles. Pulling a rubber hammer from his back pocket, he tapped each cork, leveling it with the top of the bottle.

"*E-naa*, don't leave too much space at the top, or the extra air will ruin it."

He demonstrated the proper level, corked it, and held it up. "This is how it should look, *Beeel*."

Before he left he corked more bottles to make sure we understood.

Our operation resumed, our bottles not noticeably improved. We decided to give Michel the bottles he'd corked and hide ours under the entranceway.

Because of the extra Chablis, I revisited the recycling bins but found only four bottles. After rummaging through the camper,

I came up with three plastic Evian bottles. "Do you think we can use this?" I asked, holding up a jar that held the dill pickles we'd brought back from Poland.

"Why not? Great! It even has a screw top."

"There's still too much. It'll turn sour before we can drink it all," I said.

"I'll call Bertile," Bill said, heading for the phone.

"Please, please, please, don't tell her about the pickle jar, Bill!"

When he hung up he was laughing. "She asked me what kind of wine we bought. When I told her she said, 'Sorry, I don't have any bottles for Burgundy. All my empties are for Bordeaux.'"

Would we ever learn there is a proper way to do everything in France and that using the correct shape of a bottle made a difference?

27

BALI: GOOD-BYE, 1900s

(Ina)

BILL AND I agreed Bali would be the perfect place to welcome in the twenty-first century. With all the dire warnings about computers crashing in those countries not prepared, streetlights not functioning, banks unable to dispense money, we knew such technical disruptions would slide by unnoticed in Kuta. But in case of another monsoon, we opted to stay away from the beach and find a place to live in the high part of town.

We bid adieu to the twentieth century at the Yah Yah Club. At the end of a gourmet French meal, we were given a mini version of the bamboo instruments, used by the professional orchestra from Java. Each of our mini instruments had a number to indicate the note we would play. The conductor held up fingers to signal when we should make our one-note contribution. *Yah Yah* translates as *Glorious Glorious*. We believed our rendition of "Auld Lang Syne" was nothing less.

By the end of this fourth trip, the rainfall became so heavy, the streets in the high section of town flooded. And about two weeks before we were scheduled to depart, our Mac died and couldn't be revived. Writing was out of the question for Bill, so I ventured to suggest, "Now we can do some traveling."

Bill pointed out that violent riots caused by the unsettled political and religious situations would make travel far too dangerous. His "avoiding danger" rationale didn't fit. Bill ran to danger rather than shied away from it. I then realized why he didn't want to leave—he had become friends with Usman Mirah, Indonesia's champion in both the welter and light-middleweight divisions. Bill was getting a dose of mayhem from his daily visits to a Zachariah Gym, where some of Indonesia's best boxers trained.

A few days later he told me most of the boxers were going to Jakarta by bus to see the lightweight champion fight, and Usman had invited him to accompany them. "If you'd like to go, I'm sure you'd be welcome."

How could I doubt his group of boxing friends would be other than overjoyed to have me along? Ever so sweetly I said, "That should be fun! What a great opportunity to be a part of those wild riots you mentioned are going on in Jakarta."

Bill watched the fight on TV and reported that Kuta's lightweight had won in a hard-fought match.

I did, however, get to a cremation. Bill was eager to attend since it was for Antonio Blanco, the best-known Western painter in Bali. After I left the year before, he had tea with Antonio in his gallery in nearby Ubud, Bali's cultural capital.

Since the Balinese consider death another form of life, cremations are occasions to which everyone is invited, even encouraged to attend. The locals told us his cremation would have all the trappings of a royal occasion.

We stood with several thousand people in a peaceful grassy site waiting for the arrival of the funeral procession. The crowd *oohed* when a huge, black papier-mâché bull mounted on the platform was pulled into view. Forty men strained to keep the mud-clogged wheels of the cart rolling along the soggy road.

Other men in red shirts with the name Antonio Blanco emblazoned on them hauled an eight-foot tower that carried the priest and close family members. Women attired in sarongs and sashes—obligatory for all religious occasions—and accompanied by their children walked behind a second tower covered with flowers. And last came six men carrying Antonio's body on a stretcher. Twisting and turning and occasionally walking around in circles to evade any evil spirits that might be trying to follow, they made a slow advance.

His body was transferred from the stretcher and placed inside the stomach of the black bull. After the family released a covey of white doves, the tower with the flower tributes was set alight. As the doves carried the soul of the painter off into the sky, prolonged *ahhhs* sounded from the onlookers.

And this, too, was our farewell to Bali.

(Bill)

My favorite nonstudent on Soi 13 was a twenty-four year old speech-and-hearing-impaired girl. Her mangled, half-normal-size right arm was twisted upward, yet she was usually smiling—the reason I called her Twinkle. Most of the time she wore jeans and a dirty white T-shirt. I deciphered from her sign language and limited coherent words that she slept under the overhead train tracks in a box opposite Soi 2. She offered me the keys to it more than once. I was tempted to have a look but didn't feel up to the reality.

As a break from lessons, I played a game with a partner. From a distance of about eight yards we threw tennis balls simultaneously, rapidly increasing the speed. If one of us missed, the other scored a point. Ten points made a winner. Twinkle did amazingly well. When the ball came to her good side, she seldom missed. Other times she trapped the ball against her stomach with her bad arm. We presented a curious duet in the middle of Soi 13, watching for cars and chasing the ball if we missed.

She rarely came around when I was giving lessons but sat alone on the curb about ten yards from the tables. If I asked her to join us for a beer, she would point to the 7-Eleven, where she knew beer was cheaper. I'd give her twenty bahts, and she'd return to her exile.

She bought her own beer and cigarettes when she had the money, which was most of the time. Her disability and winning smile brought in enough to keep her high.

This year she started going downhill fast. The bald spot on top of her head was getting larger, but she looked great when I said good-bye—her hair was combed over the bald spot, and she wore new tan hiking pants and a black T-shirt. We always greeted one another with hugs. I hadn't detected any fleas, but they'd be worth it.

If I get back to Soi 13, the first person I'll look for is Twinkle. I'll go to her for a big hug and hope she's still smiling.

28

Romania: Gypsy and Dracula Country

(Ina)

"Bill, you don't even know how to get there!"

"I got us to Hungary a couple of years ago, didn't I? I can find my way from there to the Ukraine."

"Yes, but since we were there, the Berlin Wall came down, and perestroika caused most everything else to change in that part of the world!"

"Neither altered the roads."

Confronted with his wisdom, I shifted my focus to the one positive: Bill had scratched Albania from his itinerary when he'd learned our insurance wasn't valid because of rampant car theft.

With the collapse of communism, lawlessness had risen exponentially. But my qualms about making this trip, which I voiced even when not given an opening, failed to dissuade Bill. He wanted to see how post-communist Eastern Bloc countries were functioning. "Have you forgotten I have a master's degree in international relations?"

I handed him a third jerrican to strap on top of the camper. We would likely need it since diesel was still in short supply in these countries.

Until we got to Hungary, Bill stuck to his plan of making our way quickly through the places we had previously visited. In Budapest he parked under a bridge by the Danube—a polluted river that bore no resemblance to the blue extolled in the waltz—to make another of his "quick trips" to buy a Hungarian language book.

"It's a difficult language," he said.

While I tried to decide which side of the bridge was the old city of Buda and which side was Pest, a policeman arrived. Since I had told Bill I thought he parked illegally, I assumed this was what he was telling me. I mimed Bill walking off but returning shortly. The second time he came, I acted out the same thing in double time. The third time, when he appeared with his ticket book and pen out, I switched tactics. I pretended I didn't know how to drive. I knew if I went zipping off and got lost on a side street, Bill and I might not be reunited. I was beginning to think that might not be such a bad idea.

We spent that night parked in front of the parliament building.

By late afternoon the next day we approached the Romanian border where lines of trucks and cars extended into the horizon—hostilities in Serbia had forced border closings so most vehicles had converged here. These drivers were of Latin temperament. If Bill didn't close any small gap within a split second, the bumper of another car wedged in.

Night came. I dozed. Bill inched. Hours later and only a few hundred yards nearer the frontier, a motorcycle policeman directed our line of cars nearer the ditch to make room for a VIP convoy. One of the cyclists, noticing our French plates, stopped to ask Bill if we would like to join the convoy. He might not have understood Bill's Romanian—it's French-Italian spoken with vigorous gestures—but he must have realized Bill's disdain for payoffs.

Hours later, still creeping, I asked, "If you're given another opportunity, will you stretch your principles?"

"If the price is still five dollars, I can be bought."

After we made it across the border, Bill pulled into a parking lot for some much-needed food and sleep. When he saw the can I was opening, he complained, "Not that again! I've been dreaming of a thick, juicy grilled steak with a baked potato and a green salad with pie for dessert."

"So have I. But it's spaghetti or nothing. But don't worry. This is our last can. From here on we eat their food!"

The minute Bill woke from his nap we took off to find those steaks. The houses we passed belonged in the backdrop of a fairy tale. Most were painted bright blue or green with white gingerbread trim. The restaurant Bill located even had a Hansel and Gretel appearance.

"Think you can decipher the menu?" I asked as the waiter ushered us to one of his many empty tables.

"Certainly! The word *bifteck* is recognizable in all Romance languages."

My question proved immaterial. The waiter came back, not with a menu, but with our food.

With a flourish he set the plate in front of us. "Mince!" he said, giving us a stainless-steel-tooth smile.

I didn't think the tennis-ball-size portion of greasy, as-yet-unidentifiable meat, accompanied by a side blob of mustard and a hard roll, merited his ostentatious presentation. It was obvious Ceausescu had followed the Russian plan—he'd developed heavy industry; agriculture had not kept pace.

Back on the road, I read that we were in Transylvania—Gypsy territory. The Romany, as they prefer being called, fled India's caste system in the fifteenth century. When they reached Europe, some became slaves. When they were freed in the mid-1800s, many remained in Romania. We saw bands of them, with hives attached to the sides of their covered wagons, ranging the countryside in search of flowers for their bees.

Bill stopped at a mountain stream to get drinking water. Bottled water is not one of the consumer items we had found.

Before I could fill our second plastic bottle a young boy dashed from behind a tree and grabbed both from my hands. He ran a few yards, stopped, slapped the bottles together, and danced, challenging Bill to catch him. Bill laughed.

At noon the next day we stopped again for steak. This restaurant's honeysuckle-covered exterior was as delightful as the first one's. Again we were ushered into the dining room and seated. The proprietor must have seen our French license plates, for he wished us "*bon appétit*" as he bowed. This time, instead of a menu, he handed us brochures written in several languages: "Within the walls of the nearby medieval citadel, you will find the Dracula House, in which Vlad Tepes, known in later life as Vlad the Impaler to some, and as Dracula to others, was born in 1431. He lived in the castle until the age of four, when his father sent him and his brother to the Turkish Sultan as hostages in an attempt to curry favor…"

I was reading, "A vampire was an undead corpse whose body didn't decay no matter how long it was in the grave" when we were served.

A tablespoon of hot mustard and a hard roll again rested beside a ball of mince.

As we ate another meal of what we now recognized as pork, I learned Vlad had executed enemies by driving a stake through their anus. And we left knowing "the local peasants' fascination with vampires became mixed with the stories of Vlad's cruelty. Bram Stoker, the British author, embroidered the legend when he wrote his novel *Dracula*."

So the werewolf of Transylvania became world entertainment, and mince became our sustenance through Romania. For a touch of variety, I alternated eggs at noon and mince at night with mince at noon and eggs at night. The word was possibly spelled and pronounced differently, but to us it remained *mince* as we minced our way toward Bucharest.

The farming scenes we passed paralleled what my father had described of his farm life in West Texas in the early 1900s. Mules pulled wagons down the furrows, and field hands weeded their crops with hoes.

At the end of their day, these farm families retired to benches outside their front-yard fence to visit with neighbors. Their gaggle of geese fed along the ditches, often straying onto the road, where the children rode bicycles without lights.

On our drive through the other countries, several people asked how much we had paid for our camper. A few asked for looks inside. In Romania not many dared dream of ever owning one. To them Bill's bicycle was the equivalent of a Rolls-Royce.

Each time we stopped, the men and boys jingled the bike's bell. They rubbed their hands along its fenders and discussed the gears. They squeezed the hand brakes. Without fail someone asked to buy it. One fellow, after showing Bill a big stack of *leu*, wasn't willing to accept Bill's "no." He followed us into a hardware store—Bill thought it prudent to buy two additional security locks. The fellow got down on his knees, placed his hands in a praying position, and upped his offer. When we pulled away, he jumped on his rickety bike, held on to a window, and rode alongside, persisting until we drove out of town.

On the outskirts of Bucharest, I yelled, "There's a pizza stand!" Bill hit the brakes and jumped out.

When he returned I asked, "What kind did you order?"

"Two of the biggest ones they had!"

I reached for the sack, eager for a look at some real food. When I ripped the paper open, a sunny-side up egg greeted me. And beneath the bright-yellow yolk…

After eating our mince pizza, Bill got a firsthand demonstration of Romanian warmth when he asked a huge, young guy where he could find the nearest bank. Instead of pointing, the fellow took firm hold of Bill's shoulders and turned him forty-five degrees to face it.

Bucharest was in a dreadful state; though we could see beauty in a few of the old buildings Ceausescu hadn't bulldozed to build a grandiose Palace of Parliament—the building he had dreamed would be the largest government building in the world. He must have considered light more important than food—the inside is decorated with hundreds of crystal chandeliers.

Neither of us saw the inside of this museum, of a church, or a store. We heard too many stories of cars being spirited across borders. Nor did we want to live on mince forever, so we took short walks, separately. My most welcome discovery was a pretzel stand. Bill went back for a batch to take with us, but, as he said, "two-day-old Romanian pretzels could serve well as building material for a retaining wall."

29

Romania: Constanta

(Ina)

"Bill, Constanta is a port city, so it will likely be even more dangerous than Bucharest." My supposition was confirmed when we arrived and Bill walked across the street to ask if the service station sold diesel. A man in a white uniform with four gold stars on each shoulder walked to the front of our van and began writing down our license number. Another pulled open Bill's door and barked, "Police!" When he said "passports," I scrambled to the back to retrieve them.

Before I had time to hand them over, Bill returned. He pushed by the fellow at the door, got in, and started the van. As we drove away, he said, "Couldn't you tell they weren't policemen?"

"No, I couldn't," I answered, though I thought it should have been obvious. After Pittsburgh and Bill's years on the road, he had enough street smarts to spot hustlers, but I had grown up in Blooming Grove, a Texas town with a population of 621. It hadn't afforded me the opportunity to learn everything.

"I don't know how much US passports are selling for, or what would have been stolen if you had opened the side door, but it would have been lucrative."

Bill must have thought it prudent to stash me where I couldn't give away our crown jewels because he located a campground and checked us in. It had two occupants plus a busload of Dutch tourists, but their restaurant had a menu posted on the door. It featured roast chicken, salad and French fries! I rejoiced, and Bill decided that menu made it worth staying a couple of days.

Even before the tour bus drove away the next morning, the owner had removed the menu, pulled down the blinds, and locked the restaurant's door.

I looked forward to seeing the Roman mosaic floors in the center of Constanta, but Bill said, "You were so right. This place is dangerous. You'd better stay here."

He, however, hopped on his bike and headed the ten kilometers back into town, where a dollar bribe got him entrance to the dock. He returned as delighted as I had seen him on any stage of this trip and reported in detail about the old ships he'd been privileged to see. "I rode up and down each dock, reading names and identifying flags. Some sailors from Senegal waved me aboard. I wheeled my bike up the gangway and shocked them with their common greeting: *"Nanga def? Jam ngaam?"* Bill said he learned this Wolof greeting, "Do you have peace?" from Senegalese friends in Paris.

The following day he drove back to Constanta for "quick" book shopping. I spent the two hours sitting in our van, surveying the action on the street. Illegal moneychangers were openly plying their trade. After I got tired of them, I watched Romany kids stealing tourist tips.

Both the timing and the cost canceled Bill's idea of taking a boat along the Black Sea to Ukraine, so he went to inquire about border crossings. Even the police seemed unaware of the best place. In utter frustration Bill broke down and bought a map.

At the first crossing, a guard issued a ten-dollar visa, but at the second barrier another guard said, "No good. You need a truck visa."

Bill said, "This is not a truck."

They sent us to a second-floor office where that clerk demanded fifty dollars for a truck fee. Bill ignored him and we waited. The clerk finally led us through a hallway and gave three timid knocks on a door before entering. With head bowed he explained the problem to his, cigar-smoking boss. The boss glared at Bill, shouted some profanity, shoved the clerk out, and slammed the door. The clerk returned to his office, took ten dollars, and threw it at Bill's feet.

We proceeded to the Moldavian border crossing, where the customs official asked, "Do you want to get killed? There's an armed revolt going on here!"

In spite of Bill's international relations degree, he was out of touch with the major events around the world.

We continued driving until we got to a Ukrainian border where we got a visa, without incident, and were off to Odessa, leaving a trail of smoke rivaling a Stanley Steamer from the diesel Bill bought from a barrel by the side of the road.

30

Ukraine: Not Too Far to Chernobyl

(Ina)

Bill hoped we were on the way to Odessa, but I couldn't match the Cyrillic letters on the Russian road signs with the letters on Bill's Romanian map. After the third crossroad, I said, "I can't help. You'll have to find the way by yourself."

We hadn't gone far before he decided I had made a wrong call. While making a U-turn, Bill noticed our fuel gauge was registering near empty. The atmosphere became tense and remained so until he spotted a station. It was across a solid line, but without the slightest hesitation Bill crossed the line. Without the slightest hesitation, a police car pulled in behind us.

"Passports and driver's license!" the policeman demanded.

Bill handed over his license. To keep me from giving our passports away, Bill had secreted them in a narrow slit between our two water tanks. By using a metal coat hanger, I could coax them within fingertip reach, but before I could extract them, they would slip back. After my sixth nervous attempt, one of the officers moved me out of the way, shone his flashlight down the slit, and made us pay a two-dollar fine.

Before the breakup of the USSR, Intourist, its all-powerful travel bureau, had dictated the route one must travel and mandated the distance to be covered each day. With these restrictions no longer in place, Bill felt confident he could stop anywhere he chose. With the food we bought at a roadside market, he decided we'd spend the night in a village a few miles off the main road. With his limited Russian—Ukrainians had been forced to study Russian in school, and the two languages are similar—he asked a man working in his garden if we could park in front of his house. The fellow insisted we come behind his iron gate so we would be safe. He further insisted that we sleep in his house. Bill was equally adamant in saying we were comfortable in our van and wouldn't think of inconveniencing his family. After removing the man's hand from his arm Bill returned to our cozy home.

By bedtime the man and his wife had given us carrots, tomatoes, and fresh strawberries. We had little to offer in return so the next morning we waited until we saw them leaving. Bill wrote a thank-you note and left them our last bottle of French wine. We bought wine in Romania that wasn't bad. In fact, it was rather good, but it didn't look impressive—it had been corked with a corncob.

Back on the main road, I was certain a sign had the word Chernobyl. "Bill, that's the site of the nuclear disaster!" The sign indicated it wasn't far off, nevertheless further on Bill insisted on a swim in the Pripyat River. My warning was dismissed. "With my wet suit, there's no danger." While he swam, I had time to realize how foolish we had been to buy that big sack of English walnuts at the roadside market. Who knew what radioactivity buzzed beneath the shells of those we had eaten? And where were the mountain streams that were so plentiful in Romania? With no bottled water here either, we had drawn our drinking water from village wells using their communal pump.

That afternoon when we stopped for the night, two young boys came by to check us out. Bill explained we were having dinner, but we planned to spend the night there. They left but returned within minutes to tell us their mother said we wouldn't be safe here and we should park in their driveway.

Bill had sworn he would never again ask for permission to park, but I insisted our safety was important. Noting there was no gate to block us in, Bill relented and followed the kids.

Their mother, Helena, quit working in her garden and persisted with her invitation to come in to see her house. I hadn't seen the first house, and Bill's details had been unsatisfactory—furnishings and floor plans make little impression on him.

She insisted we keep our shoes on, but we lined them up beside the others in her entrance room. Helena must have wanted to get to know us solo because she shooed her two wide-eyed boys and their sister out to the yard. Then, instead of showing me through her house, she seated us in armchairs in the living room and excused herself.

The room could have been in many rural homes in France—the walls were papered with flowers, and all the shelves were crammed with pictures, knickknacks, and various memorabilia.

In a few minutes a Cinderella returned—her garden clothes transformed into her Sunday best. Helena hadn't taken time for a shower after her yard work, and Bill later mentioned the incongruity of the armpit odor escaping from beneath her white ruffles. She pulled a chair across the room to communicate knee to knee with Bill. Her limited English was inferior to his faulty Russian, but they managed, and he learned she taught handicapped children.

Bill diplomatically answered, "Da," when she asked if we'd like to meet her in-laws. She sent her children, huddled by the door, across the field to fetch Pa-Pa and Ma-Ma.

They came in the living room carrying Helena's dining table covered with a white cloth, so Bill's protestations that we had eaten went ignored.

After all the food was on the table, Ma-Ma came to sit by me. She patted my face, she rubbed my arm, and she showed me the long scar on her stomach from her recent operation—gall bladder, I assumed. We couldn't converse, but we bonded. She poured me a glass of milk from the bucket she had brought with her. It was still warm from the evening milking. Though it might have meant another opportunity for me to glow in the dark, how could I refuse a gift from my soul mate?

Not to be outdone, Pa-Pa proposed a toast with a glass of his homemade vodka. Several times he demonstrated how to down the vodka in one fluid movement before sipping apple juice, also homemade.

Except for an occasional margarita, I rarely drink hard liquor. After a tentative sip of the vodka, I realized it was going to burn more if I drank it slowly, so I threw it down in his prescribed manner before gulping the apple juice. This act of self-preservation gained me more pats from Ma-Ma and a missing-teeth grin from Pa-Pa, who pronounced me "a real Ukrainian!"

After drink number one, Bill refused to play the bottoms-up game with Pa-Pa. I downed my second glass along with the others. Brilliant conversation wasn't on my agenda, and I assumed I wouldn't slur any gestures too badly.

With far more than subtle facial expressions, Pa-Pa let Bill know he wasn't "a real man." Before downing the next rounds solo, Pa-Pa patted me on the shoulder. Fortunately I wasn't pressed to drink more to uphold our family honor.

Around midnight, Petrov, Helena's husband, arrived. An hour later we were allowed to retire to our van, stuffed with cabbage, potatoes, pork, milk, and rice pudding. As a memento of our memorable evening, we carried their wedding picture along with a snapshot of the children standing in front of their house, and with several bottles of orange pop—the most popular of the soft drinks Petrov hauled. In various languages we expressed our thanks, and Bill assured them at least three times that we would write them from Paris.

Before falling asleep Bill and I agreed we'd make a very early start. The night had been an experience we would remember, but everything we thought needed to be said had been said, more than once.

We woke to find Petrov had moved his truck. It was now blocking the driveway.

Again we sat in our armchairs. Again the table was brought in. Petrov apologized profusely because there was no more vodka. Bill searched the camper and found part of a bottle of crème de menthe. Eager to taste this new green liquid, Petrov had his glass to his lips almost in unison with his Ukrainian "to your health!" I skipped the alcohol to focus on downing my large bowl of rice swimming in Ma-Ma's unpasteurized milk.

After breakfast Helena handed Bill an envelope containing several bills of Ukrainian script—the temporary currency they used until they could print their own. *Did she want us to send them something from Paris?* I wondered. Bill explained later that it was a parting gift.

Assuring them we had changed money at the border, Bill was in the middle of saying, "This is such a thoughtful gesture, but—" In midsentence all eyes shifted from him to *Maria*, the Mexican soap opera that was wreaking havoc throughout the former Soviet Union. En masse workers called in sick not to miss a single episode. *Maria* was indeed high drama, and we blessed her for our long respite. All eyes, including the children's, were welded on every frame of her emotional, heart-wrenching saga—none of which I could understand.

After a thorough discussion of the episode and what I assumed was speculation about what would happen next, we again became part of the family's lives. Eventually we were allowed to take our leave—after hugs and kisses accompanied by heaped-on pleas to stop by on our return from Odessa. Petrov moved his truck, while Helena and her brood followed us out the door. Her parting gesture was to stuff the envelope with the Ukrainian script in Bill's pocket.

"Free at last! Thank God in heaven, I'm free at last," Bill said as he drove off. As we turned to enter the main highway, a hay wagon was blocking the road. There was Pa-Pa, one hand yanking on the reins, the other hand motioning for us to stop.

"He probably forked the hay at about six in the morning," Bill said.

"He certainly looks fresh!" I added.

He jumped down to give me a big bear hug. Bill got a limp handshake and an ultimatum to bring me back for another visit.

Bill had his own ultimatum when we left: "No matter what, we're only sleeping in designated areas from now on."

Of course, this turned out to be a colossal mistake.

31

Ukraine: On to Odessa

(Bill)

Driving into Odessa, I followed the leftover Intourist signs through the winding streets to the campground, where a guard with a German shepherd raised the bar. At the office I paid twelve US dollars—exorbitant in Ukraine's current economic condition—then drove around a circular road to the middle of a grassy area near the toilets. One trailer was the only thing in this big campground.

While Ina checked out the facilities, I branched into their electric line.

The guard and his police dog interrupted me. "You stay?" the guard asked in English.

"Yeah," I said. "I paid twelve dollars for this place."

"If you want to be safe, you should offer a little something to me."

"And what would that 'little something' be?"

"Five dollars."

I shouted an unprintable profanity and stormed to the office. "What the hell kind of place is this? I paid twelve dollars for this dump. My wife tells me there's no hot water and no lock on the toilet door or a light in there, and now the guard is threatening me to get a bribe."

"Oh, I'm sure you misunderstood," the secretary said, "I'll call the manager."

The manager went with me to the gate to confront the guard, who denied my charge.

The manager said, "He doesn't understand a word you're saying."

"He understands exactly what I'm saying." My emotion must have incited the police dog. He snarled and the manager had to grab his collar. "Shut your mouth and go back to your van," he shouted.

I went, but not without adding, "This place is worse than Chicago in the Capone days."

At least that broke the tension—it elicited a smile.

I was afraid the guard might spread the word to the drunken Ukrainians, who were whooping it up in an adjoining dance hall, so I stayed awake with a lead bar and a tear gas sprayer beside me.

At first light I left and drove until I saw a fenced-off area in a secure-looking spot overlooking the Black Sea. There was a boat and a car, but room for our van. The owner was delighted with my offer of five dollars a night.

We attracted a lot of attention. One of the manager's friends gave us a nice bass and insisted on cleaning and grilling it for us. We were truly impressed by the kindness of most of the Ukrainians.

The highlight for me was the port, even though I couldn't sneak into any of the gates because of the dispute over which country owned the subs, cruisers, and destroyers of the former Soviet Union.

The first day we went into the city center I asked several people where to find a restaurant. No one knew since few had the money to eat out. They could only point us in the direction of the long-standing Intourist establishment where the prices were at least three times the going rate for both food and rooms. But directly across the street was a restaurant with a menu that filled a whole page.

We alternated ordering red with black caviar before fish, or anything other than pork.

After dinner we would visit the free market, where refined older ladies sold their jewelry for much less than its value. I did feel sorry for the ladies—they must have had strong emotional attachments to their jewelry—but I didn't feel guilty about the high black-market exchange rate I got.

After leaving Odessa, we retraced our route, but I made sure it was at a time when Pa-Pa wouldn't catch me again.

Our next stop was Kiev, a capital with a rich history. We didn't stay, though I did manage an hour of people watching; and we purchased several jars of caviar.

Another pileup delayed us at the Ukrainian border. Every Polish car was being strip-searched. They had to take out every article, including mattresses. The guards patted them down for hidden merchandise, as most Europeans know the Poles are very adept at outwitting any custom agent.

Several days later, when I finally turned onto our street in Port Marly, Ina let out a sigh. "*Le Bienveillant* has never looked better to me," she said.

I unpacked the van, which now carried an inflatable official USSR naval rubber raft I had bought at Odessa's free market, though Ina kept saying, "We don't need it! It will never be used. Our motorboat is safer."

Of course I would prove her wrong. I'd get Michel to inflate it and take us for a ride before I gave it to him.

"It's been a long trip in a confined space," Ina said, "but I did get to meet my soul mate. And while I babysat the camper, I did these." She held up the two supersized Christmas stockings she had cross-stitched.

32

VIETNAM: HO CHI MINH CITY

(Ina)

BILL CHOSE THE corner café/restaurant on the liveliest budget travelers' street in Ho Chi Minh City to set up his language exchange. Around the corner was the Sinh Café, the place backpackers went to swap travel stories, get information, and book tours.

Most days I waited in line at the bank across the street. With an exchange rate of more than eleven thousand dongs to the dollar we were dong billionaires; yet few merchants would accept a bill larger than a twenty. Exchanging big dongs for little dongs became a regular necessity—there was a limit on the low denominations we could get at one time.

The first time I saw the courier arrive, he was sitting behind the motorcycle driver holding on to a two-and-a-half foot stack of little dongs. It was astounding. He swayed, but kept one hand firmly on the bottom of the stack and the other glued to the top. He held on to nothing other than this as they zoomed through the dense motorcycle traffic.

On our first night, Bill got acquainted with the kids who roamed the streets selling peanuts, postcards, candy—whatever they could get their hands on. Bill asked one who peddled guidebooks if he had a new *Rough Guide to Vietnam*.

"I bring one tomorrow," he promised. "Only two dollars! Vietnam number one in photocopies."

Then there was Bo, a twelve-year-old who slept on the sidewalk in front of the café. He begged for food by doing rapid, three-finger pats on his open mouth. It didn't take Bo long to latch on to Bill. And Bill, assuming it would serve as the proverbial learning to catch a fish, bought him a lock-up, fully equipped shoeshine box.

Bo work? Not a chance. However, he found a use for his new box: he locked the money he hustled inside and paid the waiter at the restaurant to keep it safe.

Word travels fast, and resourceful kids began sketching our portraits. They handed Bill their drawings, their expressions indicating they weren't expecting praise for their artistic endeavors. Bo also made stick figure drawings of us. I didn't need a professional to interpret Bill's pumpkin smile and my wicked sneer.

Though I'll admit my disposition wasn't the greatest, I knew Bo's portrayal was prompted by jealousy. Each time I visited the ice cream parlor across the street, Bill had to hold my hand to lead me through the dense motorcycle traffic. Bo invariably ran between us to break us apart. His feelings for me were the least of my concern, but when Bill asked, "Why are you being so bitchy?" I realized I needed to do some serious introspection.

Bill's question was justified, but I had no explanation. I couldn't pinpoint what was bothering me. I had looked forward to this trip. Our American friends had raved about their tours here. And according to the French, Vietnam was the "in place" to visit this year. Although I had anticipated encountering some hostility—one reason we traveled with our Irish passports—we encountered none. Some Vietnamese went out of their way to tell us how great America is.

What was my problem? Was it because we were staying in one place, learning about life on this corner?

To Bill everything there was exciting. He wasn't the least bit perturbed on the night two policemen barged into our room at three in the morning asking, "How many people are sleeping here." They gave no explanation and left when Bill answered their question. I suppose they hoped to discover extras so they could collect a fine.

Won, the girl in charge of the ice cream parlor across the street, planned to teach American—as the Vietnamese insisted on calling our language—when she finished college. She spoke well, but she pronounced *P* as *B*. I had her hold her hand in front of my mouth to feel the difference, but that didn't cure her problem. She wanted to practice her American, and I wanted to learn about the happenings on Bill's corner, so we agreed on an exchange—conversation for her, information for me.

The story the kids roaming the streets at night told Bill was. "I have to sell things, or my family won't have enough to eat." I first asked her about that.

"Oh, they just like to be out because it's more fun than staying home. They use their tourist money to buy fun things. They have blenty to eat."

"What about that legless, handless man who pushes himself around on a flat board with his stubby arms? Does he collect enough to feed himself?"

She laughed at this question. "He's the richest man in our neighborhood. His wife sbends all day gambling with what he collects."

Many kids who circulated during the day told heart-wrenching stories about not having the money to attend school.

"Our schools are free," she said, "but if both barents work, there's no one home to make them go."

She also told me the government would provide Bo with a place to sleep, but he, like so many others, preferred the street because government dorms were too far "from the action."

In this hot, steamy climate, I hadn't managed to get any exercise. Both my body and mind cried for the release it might provide, so I asked Won for recommendations of places to walk.

She was horrified. "Oh, you mustn't walk if you have the money to ride. It's not right!"

I was willing to buck this cultural no-no, but crossing a street was scary. People lived five to a room and pooled their earnings to save enough to buy a motorcycle, so motorcycles were everywhere. But I was determined. As I walked away from the tourist street, I enjoyed the passing parade of styles. The Vietnamese girls were fashion conscious. They wore white, above-the-elbow gloves and original hats decorated with flowers, feathers, and everyday objects, such as feather dusters. The woman I found particularly creative wore a tin funnel with the spout holding a bouquet of multicolored flowers.

I planned my route to take advantage of the one set of traffic lights I knew existed. But in the split second it took the light to change, one cluster of motorcycles peeled off to the left, another to the right, and the largest group barreled through the intersection. I waited through several light changes, hoping to find some way to use the light to my advantage to cross the street. I was on the verge of giving up when a grandmother with a walking stick took me by the arm and stepped out in the street with me in tow. She walked with a steady, measured step, looking neither to the right nor to the left, only straight ahead. The bikers swerved around us.

The sights on the other side interested me, so whenever something piqued my curiosity—a shop window or a new type of flower or an old man just sitting, talking to his caged bird—I stopped. Hours later, with no idea how to get back to the boulevard, I asked a young man for directions—many young people spoke American—and he offered to take me to my hotel. Though, after surviving my Thailand ride with Bill, I'd made that solemn promise never again to get on a motorcycle, I weighed the odds of having the nerve to cross that boulevard again. I accepted the young man's offer.

Bill was outside looking for me. When he saw me arrive, holding tight to my deliverer, he must have realized my problem was indeed serious.

The next day we took a pedicab to a shopping area. We were both browsing in a busy market when I called out, "Bill, he's got his hand in your backpack." Bill turned to see a little fellow disappear into the crowd.

Thirty minutes later a stocky guy tapped Bill on the shoulder and handed him his expired Irish passport—I have no idea why Bill carried it. The little one stood off to the side.

"Thanks," Bill said.

"Give me a dollar," the fellow demanded.

"What?"

"Give me a dollar!" he repeated.

With people sitting at sidewalk cafés, Bill must have felt safe in pointing to the sky and telling him in explicit terms what to do to the moon.

The man made a threatening gesture before disappearing.

Bill smiled. "That's not only chutzpah. It's survival pushed to the limit."

During my next conversation with Won, I asked what disease caused the bleeding, open sores we saw on the beggars at the market.

"Oh." She giggled. "They don't have a disease. They use some kind of jelly stuff to make it look like they're wounded so tourists will feel sorry and give them money."

Like many others, Bill had dispensed dongs to aid those we'd thought were destitute. He now became more judicious with his handouts. He chose a Cambodian woman as the recipient of his charity after Won told me, "Our neighborhood takes care of most beople who need help, but she has a hard time. Many don't like her because she's not one of us."

The Cambodian sat in the same doorway each evening, holding her baby. Won said she had married an American who had left when he'd discovered she had TB. Each night Bill gave her money and treated her and her baby to ice cream. Three nights before we left, she wasn't in her doorway and didn't reappear. We assumed she was too sick to get there.

In another couple of days, Bill hired a cyclo, a three-wheeled cart, so he could take me to other parts of the city. The three-story churches with a different symbol on each floor raised my curiosity. I knew the government frowned on organized religion, though

Won said many Vietnamese professed to follow a type of Buddhism mixed with animism, ancestor worship, Taoism, Confucianism, and a large dose of superstitions. I learned this church with a giant eye was for a combination of religious and nationalist movements. Among their saints were Brahma, Moses, Joan of Arc, Victor Hugo, and Sun Yat-sen.

Again, nothing here seemed straightforward to me.

The day I admired Won's new purple silk slacks, she offered to take me to the market. "You must have new clothes for Tết. It's pad luck not to have new clothes for the New Year."

Won lived with her brother, his wife, and their two young children in a one-bedroom apartment. Her brother had inherited the money when their father died, so she was his responsibility until she married. Won arranged for the use of her family's motorbike, and the next day before work she wove me through crosstown traffic to her sister's shop, where I was measured for the new clothes I hoped would ward off bad luck. I paid the tourist price for the silk at the market, but my theory that everyone in this country was out for money was lessened when Won's sister charged the extremely low Vietnamese price for her sewing. I had to insist the extra money was a Tết bonus.

Bill learned many travelers visited the secret tunnels on the outskirts of Saigon. Neither of us was interested in tunnels, so we went to the war memorial museum instead. There we received this brochure:

> In 1965, with a gigantic force involving 6 million turns of soldiers, the United States began launching a year of aggression against Vietnam. In early 1969 US military forces in South Vietnam amounted to 543,400 men, not counting 70,000 soldiers of contingents coming from some US "Allies" plus nearly a million troops of the Saigon regime. For years, US planes dropped 7,850,000 tons of bombs and sprayed 75 million liters of lethal chemicals on villages, rice fields, and forests in South Vietnam.

The above-mentioned figures do not include huge amounts of gun shells and other kinds of bullets shot by US troops and "Allies" soldiers. Atrocious crimes were committed against the Vietnamese, particularly the 1958 Son My (My Lai) massacre. B52s carried out carpet-bombing on densely populated areas including Hanoi and major cities and towns of North Vietnam. World public opinion condemned the US for making full use of sophisticated weapons against Vietnam. It was known that the US government spent 352 billion dollars on the Vietnam War ending in 1975 and that Vietnam has been suffering tremendous consequences from it.

Uncountable invalids for life, foetus malformations, and body deformities, especially in babies, have been observed by scientists. Until now, orchards and forests heavily damaged by chemicals during the long war have hardly been recovered. Vietnam has suffered from countless losses in economic, cultural, and social activities.

The Americans were deeply shocked at the war in Vietnam. In consecutive years protests against the war were staged by different walks of life in the US as well as in other parts of the globe. The Vietnamese are grateful to the people around the world, especially the Americans, for having helped them struggle for independence, freedom, and happiness in Vietnam.

After reading this I again experienced the paradox I'd felt since I arrived. They seemed to be making a distinction between the United States and Americans. Were they saying things to please all persuasions? Again, I couldn't put things in a frame of reference. I didn't understand.

I looked at only a few pictures of massacred bodies and the devastation Agent Orange caused before leaving the museum to sit on one of the benches in the courtyard and wait for Bill. I'm usually able to keep from displaying my emotions so openly, but this time my sobs were audible.

The Vietnamese man next to me leaned over. "Did you lose someone special here?" he asked.

I shook my head before I realized we all—Vietnamese, Americans, and our allies—had lost someone or something special here.

After two weeks we said our good-byes to the ice cream girls. When Bill assured them, "We'll see you next year around this same time," my stomach tightened. I didn't want to come back.

33

Vietnam: "Not Saigon Again!"

(Ina)

We planned to take trains, but they were booked solid, so we took the Sinh Café's mini bus to Nha Trang, the first stop on our way to Hanoi. Bill had swimming in mind, and I looked forward to quiet walks on the beach.

I should have suspected that neither the weather nor the water would cooperate.

During Bill's first swim, a wave knocked off one of his flippers. He bought a Russian pair at a market, and tied them on. They stayed in place, but the waves hit with such force and unpredictability, he was lucky to make it back to shore. As he struggled out of the water, the Frenchman who sold diving equipment came running down, shouting, "Are you out of your mind? Can't you see nobody is swimming in this surf?"

Then heavy daily rain began pounding. The only prediction of good weather for the next couple of weeks was in the Mekong Delta, which required a return to Ho Chi Minh City.

On arrival back at the Sinh Café, I said, "Bill, remember how excited you were about that snake farm you heard about? It's just south of here." Even snakes were preferable to spending more time here. Bill was excited so we boarded another minibus.

Bill took his time learning about the snakes and especially one that kept hurling itself against the cage when anyone walked past. "Oh, he chases people," we heard one guide say. "If he goes after you, stop and turn around. He won't follow if you run against wind. Even if he catches you, he not poison."

This triggered other questions, but I didn't stay for the snake answers. I was puzzled by strange membranes hanging from nearby wires to dry. I went to investigate.

"You want buy kidney medicine?" the seller asked. "I fill my snake bladders with their bile. You got problem? It cure."

I had a few, but more bile wasn't what I needed.

Bill learned from a Belgian girl about a floating market nearby. After making a complete round of the snakes, with a second look at the chaser, Bill asked where to find the dock she'd mentioned.

We joined five other passengers on one of the small, open boats transporting people along various branches of the Mekong. It was hard to imagine what the people we passed were thinking. From under the shade of their conical straw hats, they watched intently until we were out of sight. Some smiled; more stared, expressionless.

We heard squealing pigs, squawking chickens, and especially the honking of geese. The vendors' boats—often powered by old steam engines or automobile motors—most often were a vibrant yellow, blue, red, or a combination of colors. A bunch of bananas, a watermelon, bundles of sugarcane, baskets of coconuts—whatever they had for sale—dangled from a bamboo stalk bending over the bow. The boatmen displayed the same dexterity as motorcyclists, maneuvering their boats within inches of each other.

The buyers, however, used long poles to push their boats.

After only an hour, Bill said, "Enough. We both need a rest. Let's find a beach."

When our restaurant waiter finished explaining about his undiscovered beach on the Gulf of Siam, I asked, "Bill, do you think he's right?"

"Sure. He lives there, so he knows what he's talking about."

Comprehending directions is a problem for both of us. In Vietnam we found it more so. Whether Bill spoke American or French—his version of Vietnamese was useless—we always missed a few salient facts. Since we would be venturing into the unknown, Bill had the waiter repeat the instructions three times. Even then we agreed on only two points: "It's a short trip" and "The bus leaves at ten o'clock at night."

To ensure we had seats, we arrived at the bus station at nine fifteen. When we located our bus, I looked it over.

"It's something like the ones I rode to school, but I don't think De Soto made our buses."

De Soto hadn't made this bus either. It was a hybrid—various parts had been welded together to make it. De Soto simply happened to be the name displayed on the grille.

A young fellow hefted our backpacks on top, and Mama Ticket Taker seated us up front behind the driver. Ten o'clock came. Only one other passenger had arrived, so we waited. Around midnight, when several more people boarded, all seven of the male passengers were motioned off to push our bus until it got started.

When the motor caught, the men scrambled back aboard. The driver didn't want to risk stalling, so when passengers wanted off, he slowed down enough for the young fellow, who also handled the baggage, to hurry them off. He also pulled new passengers aboard.

With a low battery, our headlights were dim, so this same young man leaned out the open door while holding on to a bar. His "Yip, yip, yip!" chased the chickens and cows off the road. We assumed his high-and low-toned sounds told the driver which direction to swerve to avoid potholes, though this wasn't confirmed since we hit quite a few.

These rather constant sounds kept me awake. I complained about our driver speeding, but Bill assured me, "We aren't going over thirty." Even thirty taxed the motor, and steam began to seep out around our feet. I collected my belongings to move to the back, but one of the two extra drivers/mechanics motioned for me to remain.

He calmly pulled up the floorboards, and though the bus never stopped, he and his partner worked on the motor. They kept jerking their hands back to escape the steam as one taped a piece of leather around the rusting pipes. The steam quit seeping, but in less than an hour, it began billowing. This time the driver stopped. His shouts and frantic waving sent everyone scrambling off.

We drank coffee at an all-night stand as we watched water being directed along the hot pipes and into the radiator. Bill worried the water would hit the sizzling block and crack it.

"Look," he said, poking me awake. "Now they're filling the barrel on the roof."

This oversized barrel was not only supplying water for the nonfunctioning water pump. Its drips had made mud pies in my dust-covered hair.

Repairs complete, the driver waved the women back on board. Bill again helped the men push the bus to get us started, and we were back on our way.

Sometime around six o'clock, Mama Ticket Taker woke us, and we were herded off the bus onto the side of the road. Our backpacks came hurtling down from the roof.

"I can smell the beach," Bill said. "That fellow was right. It wasn't far."

Though I was still sleepy, I saw no beach, but I did recognize the sound of motorcycles zooming up the road. They screeched to a stop in front of us. One driver grabbed my backpack. By that time climbing on a motorcycle had become routine. The new experience was having my heavy pack strapped to my back while sitting on the motorcycle. Off we flew, me hanging on with such intensity that I would have taken the driver with me had I become dislodged.

"Did you see that beautiful sunrise?" Bill asked forty minutes later as he helped me and my backpack dismount. "It was one of the prettiest I've ever seen."

"You know, I think I missed it." My head had been buried in the driver's back as we'd bounced over bumps and swerved around holes. At least I now knew why this was an undiscovered beach.

We slept for a good part of the day. That night, although there wasn't a single streetlight, Bill said, "Let's explore."

The grunting I heard didn't prepare me for a drift of hogs rushing down the road. Our collision with them terminated our first outing.

The next day after a swim, we took a five-minute walk to the edge of town and back. Bill stopped by the square to join some women for a bingo-type game. "At a penny a card, this is a cheap way for me to learn numbers," he said.

While he played, the women examined my wristwatch and freckles. They seemed intrigued by both. After Bill became proficient enough to take a turn calling games, I left. My hair needed attention.

At the beauty shop, I stepped over the ubiquitous sow—a pregnant one sunning in the doorway. When I used sign language to express my desire, the woman dragged an ordinary chair into the middle of her dirt floor. I had been in Vietnam long enough to know I was to sit up straight for the soaping part. I still didn't know why they collected the soap bubbles in a bowl and set it aside. But being both frugal and ingenious, I figured they most likely knew a way to recycle bubbles.

Not until the rinse was my head pulled back. As the water ran out on the dirt floor, I raised my feet. I was afraid the sow would move from the doorway to wallow in the wet spot. The water was cold, but the neck and head massage made my five-cent shampoo another unforgettable experience.

While talking with the waiter and waitress at our hotel, we were told, "To land good job, we must speak American, know computers, and own a motorcycle." These particular young people struggled with the first requirement. Our supposition that all those learning American used the same textbook was confirmed. We became adept at knowing which sections they had covered by the phrases used. "What is your name?" meant the beginning pages of book one. "What countries have you visited?" signified they were near the middle. "How old are you?" and "How many sons do you have?" signified nothing. Everyone who spoke any sort of American asked this.

The music coming over the loudspeakers at 5:00 a.m., along with vigorous counting as workers did government-mandated calisthenics, was no longer the novelty it had been. And, after a few days of swimming in warm water, Bill said it was time to return to Saigon to catch trains to Hanoi.

While checking for a bus to get us out of town, he discovered a twelve-hour boat trip along the Cambodian border. "After all," he said, "it will take us only a few miles out of our way, and another day or so won't matter."

This time a real bus deposited us at the dock. When families arrived, they slung their hammocks along the beam running the length of the boat and then settled back to nap or eat. Several people vacated their hammocks to talk with Bill, who was already exchanging lessons up front. When they insisted I take their place, I accepted. Not only was it relaxing to sway, I learned the young couple sitting near me had borrowed money to buy the little pig the young man was holding. They planned to fatten it and use the profit from its sale to finance their wedding.

Once again it was back to the Sinh Café to take their minibus. With Tết nearing, people were flocking home to be with their families so trains were fully booked.

We first traveled back to Nha Trang, with our knees pressed against the seat in front of us. From there we took regular buses heading north. Our stop at Hội An for Tết proved special. During the seventeenth century, Hội An had been one of the important port cities in Southeast Asia. Merchant ships from around the world sailed up the river that connected it with the South China Sea. Long ago sand had silted this port, but otherwise the old picturesque quarter had scarcely changed.

Everyone in Hội An seemed to be holding open house. As we walked along, we were beckoned inside to see family altars. People gave us handfuls of watermelon seeds they had dyed red for luck. Children pressed "lucky money" coins in our hands. We were afraid they expected the lucky money we gave them in exchange should be the paper variety. When we ran out of our little dongs, we beat a fast retreat—we didn't want to spoil the spirit of their celebration.

When we walked over the covered wooden bridge the Japanese community had built in the sixteenth century, we met the woman who had told Bill about Hội An when they had exchanged lessons in Saigon. She invited us to lunch the next day.

A downpour was pinging the roof as we prepared to leave. We didn't have an umbrella and weren't near a store selling them.

Me: (Approaching the girl at our hotel desk.) Do you have an extra umbrella we could borrow for a couple of hours?

Her: (With a big smile.) Oh, yes! (Returning from the storeroom, she held it up.) Is only one.

Bill: No problem. We can both use the same one.

Her: Is only one! (Still smiling, she turned to replace the umbrella from whence it came.)

The Vietnamese reluctance to say "no" has no bounds.

We scrounged for a piece of plastic to hold over our heads. When we arrived, Bill's former student introduced her boyfriend. He was a French fellow who exported teak furniture to a warehouse within walking distance of our houseboat. He and Bill talked about a restaurant owner they both knew in Saint-Germain. The lunch was delicious—my first proof that Vietnamese chickens had meat on their bones. We hadn't discovered the food we appreciated in their restaurants in Paris.

Our minibuses stopped at Da Nang and Hué on our way to the Gulf of Tonkin. But even the Sinh Café's tourist buses didn't make the final leg due to poor road conditions, so we flew into Hanoi, a city set back in time. Its French colonial buildings on wide boulevards were not unlike Paris. The population here was older, and the mentality was different from Saigon. Here, the traffic lights were also for pedestrian use.

All the karaoke bars closed during Tết, and signboards displaying females with low-cut blouses or revealing skirts were removed. Our two young hotel night clerks didn't approve of these crackdowns. One closed the shutters on the front windows. The other put his finger to his lips before he unwrapped and then proudly played a Michael Jackson video he'd hidden in the back of a closet.

When we began packing to fly back to Thailand, Bill said, "You weren't the only one who didn't like Saigon. Every woman I talked with felt the same. Besides, I know you aren't a bitcher at heart. We'll go somewhere else for Tết next year."

When he failed to pack his Vietnamese language books, I knew this meant I wouldn't be coming back to resolve my feelings about the people or the country. Survival was the word I felt best described how they were living. Yet I left knowing that with their ingenuity, Vietnam would evolve into whatever her people wanted her to be. And that was exactly as it should be!

34

Morocco: Couscous and Camels

(Ina)

It was April in Paris, and chestnuts were in blossom, but the rains that fell were more than gentle showers. After weighing the pros and cons of driving to either Italy or Greece for some sun, we settled on Sicily, a place we hadn't visited. Bill left to buy a guidebook. Before he got to the bookstore, he found a bargain flight to Morocco, so we switched continents.

On arrival in Marrakech, we checked into to Hotel Ali, recommended by our Aussie boat friends as a great bargain. Most evenings we served ourselves from its ten steaming ceramic pots, ladling an array of vegetables and lamb, chicken, and *merguez* onto our plates. Bill covered his serving with more than enough of the pungent red *harrisa* hot sauce. We rounded out our couscous meal with fruit and pastries we chose from a different table. Wine was on the table.

The other highlight at the Hotel Ali was its rooftop terrace. Young backpackers paid a nominal price to camp on the roof, where they had a view of Djemaa el-Fnna, the plaza and the heart of Marrakech. Although it was primarily a gathering place for the

Berbers who came in from the surrounding desert, it was also the number one draw for foreigners.

On our first night, we were astounded to see women marching around the plaza, carrying placards. Though women had gotten the right to vote when the king granted it to men a few years after Morocco received her independence from France, their public participation in politics had never been overt. Politics was for men, not women. Even now they weren't making a complete break with Muslim tradition—they still wore their caftans, and one was veiled. Yet atop each beautiful scarf perched a hot-pink baseball cap.

"Bill, find out why they're marching," I urged.

He tried, but the men waved him away, refusing to discuss the matter. He eventually learned that the caps were the symbol of a left-wing political party.

Bill and I settled into a routine. He collected words from the boys shining shoes in the square in front of our hotel. He didn't make much progress with his Arabic—spoken Moroccan is a dialect. Sometimes he could communicate without using French because modern Arabic is used on the TV and in films.

I spent much of my days sitting under the Ali's covered terrace, either reading or talking with the constant flow of tourists. Peace Corps volunteers had come to soak up what they considered luxuries at the conclusion of a two-year stint in Mali. Other rugged individuals came to mountain climb in the High Atlas range. Several Christians were surreptitiously passing out New Testaments. And college students came for cross-cultural credits.

The Hotel Ali was a good place to see the Moroccans' religion in action. The Moroccans' faith permeated their public and private lives. It was near the Koutoubia minaret, so we heard the call to prayer five times a day. We were also near the madrasa, the university annex where students lived when they came to study and memorize the Koran.

On our third night, after Bill finished an Arabic lesson with the waiter, I said, "More than half the people I meet have taken camel rides into the Sahara where they spend the night in tents."

"That sounds different," Bill said. "We should try it."

We joined a group of eight young people for a scenic minibus ride across the Atlas Mountains to the Sahara. On the way I sat by two Japanese girls who introduced me to the care and feeding of their Tamagotchi, the mechanical pet that was all the rage that year. They had kept their dog "alive" for twenty-three days.

During our lunch stop, we examined some impressive fossils. The manager warned us, "Be careful you don't buy those fakes for sale at the *souks* in Marrakech. You need to take a knife to test for plaster if you go there. Here there's no need to worry. Mine are all authentic."

Before we reached our rendezvous, our young entourage bought complete outfits of desert garb: baggy pants, scarves or *burnooses*, and yellow *babouches*, those open-at-the-heel shoes. Outfitted for roles as sheiks of the burning sand, they were ready for the next step, which was to choose a camel.

The group insisted I select mine first. I remembered daddy checked the teeth of a horse for something. All the camels seemed to have impervious smirks that covered their dental work, so I chose the one with the thickest rugs.

When everyone was ready, Massoud, our guide, ordered the camels to kneel, and we climbed aboard. He held the reins of the lead camel to walk us single file into the desert as the sun began sinking into the horizon. Naturally Bill had selected a spunky camel that foamed at the mouth. The spittle soon disturbed the German girl who was behind him. When she complained, the guide relegated Bill to the back of the line, but placated him by saying, "You have chosen a young one looking for some action."

That evening, while Massoud prepared *kabobs* over a charcoal brazier, he entertained us with Berber lore. This was my favorite story:

> A Berber boy looks over all the girls when he walks around town. When he sees one who catches his eye, he tells his mother. If, after investigating the

girl's character, Mother thinks the girl and her son will be compatible, she engages a marriage broker to negotiate.

After the marriage broker reaches a satisfactory agreement, the bride's mother invites the boy and his mother to their home. While they wait for tea, she asks probing questions, hoping to pry loose stray information about her daughter's prospective husband.

Teatime is the moment of suspense. With the first sip, the boy and his mother will know if he and the girl will be exchanging rugs, symbolizing their engagement. If their tea is not sweetened, he'll have to take another look at the girls walking around the town.

Our evening ended with everyone gyrating to the music of a reed flute and a drum. I woke several hours later, needing to make a trip outside our communal tent. I was fearful of what creepy-crawly creatures lurked in the sand, though I doubted snakes would be up and about in the cool night air. I waited as long as I could before easing out of my sleeping bag, slipping on shoes I hoped would offer protection. I crept out of the tent as quietly as possible. Two of the other three females had obviously been waiting for someone to make the first move, so they joined me. One had stripped her bed twice looking for scorpions before she lay down, so I knew she wasn't making this trip by choice either.

We headed for the nearest sand dune. On my way back, I looked up at the night sky. Never before had I seen so many stars! Nor had I seen them sparkling with such brilliance in a black-velvet sky…accompanied by the howls of jackals.

The next morning the sun was already hot by the time we were ready to return. Bill bought a white tablecloth from Massoud and draped it under my hat and around my shoulders. I might not have been as stylish as the young people with their burnooses, but I was better protected.

One member of our group thought he knew everything about every movie ever made, so on our return trip, he persuaded the bus driver to take us by a desert movie set near Quarzazate.

"Bill, have you heard of any those movies?" I asked as we climbed the steep hill to view the elaborate, columned construction used in several films about ancient Egypt.

"Not unless he mentioned *Lawrence of Arabia*, I haven't."

We clamored over the dunes, getting covered with sand.

The minute we returned to Marrakech, I went in search of a beauty salon. Though most tourists seek out shops in the foreign quarter, I like to learn how the locals operate, so I found an upstairs establishment overlooking the plaza. When I sat down, I apologized because my hair was so filled with sand.

"No problem," the young girl assured me as she wet my hair with cold water. She squirted on some shampoo from what looked like a red plastic ketchup bottle. Then she raked a brush through it a couple of times, ran a little more cold water over it, and escorted me to the barber chair for my haircut.

Oh well, I thought. *I can always shampoo again. What I really need is a haircut.* I negotiated the amount to be cut and scrunched down so she could reach me better—the adjustment on the chair didn't work. She began dancing to the music floating up from the plaza and was obviously paying more attention to her dancing than to her cutting, for she whacked off large clumps, not the negotiated amount. I straightened up. After one look in the mirror, I scrunched back down. I had no choice but to let her cut the other side. *Oh well. It grows fast.*

"Non, non, non," I said, rising from the chair again. "I don't want to have it blow-dried. I don't need any more heat on it."

"*Oui, oui, oui,*" she insisted as she pushed me back down in the nonadjustable chair.

Oh well. When in Rome...At that point what did one more fiasco matter?

After my nonshampoo, a scalping, and a bouffant blow-dry that teased my remaining locks into standing on end, my beauty operator stood back for a long, hard appraisal. Keeping her eye on me, she backed over to her personal makeup kit. After rummaging around in it, she came back with her bright-red lipstick and painted me a glossy, pouting mouth.

The only "oh well" I could think of was: *Bill will probably say he can try to get me a job as a lady of the night.*

After a couple of weeks in Marrakech, we took a local bus to Essaouira, an old port city. It was windy—at least that pleased the surfers. The city, formerly called Mogador, had eighteenth-century ramparts the Portuguese had built. Some of their old cannons still faced the Atlantic.

Bill got us a room in a hotel built into the city wall. It had seen better days, but the terrace roof garden faced the ocean. As expected, he headed for the port to look over the small fishing fleet. When he returned, he was bubbling.

"They were like boats from years back. They had large crews, all the lines were hemp, and three sailors were patching nets, while others were chipping rusty winches.

"Sorry I missed those rusty winches."

"There's an open-air restaurant at the dock. We can choose from their latest catch and watch them cook it."

While we ate grilled calamari, we tried to identify the fish that came sliding down the ramp from a nearby boat. We didn't have much luck. The vendors covered them with ice too quickly.

Europeans often come here to look for property to buy for winter homes, and this was the project of the French fellow who was staying at our hotel. Poor Didier was a perpetual loser. Nothing he tried panned out. The resident dog snarled at him each time he left the hotel. A man in a nearby souvenir shop accused him of propositioning his younger sister—they nearly came to blows. Our cook, the manager, and the Moroccan visitors all disliked Didier. His two property deals fell through—the house he wanted flooded during his second visit, and he backed out of the other when the owner tried to raise the price after he was prepared to sign. Poor

Didier didn't seem to belong in Morocco, though, as Bill said, "I'm not sure where he belongs."

Daily we listened to his latest misfortune. His only triumph was the selection of vegetables he'd bought at a market for two francs. Each day we received a lecture about how to eat "for next to nothing." Didier was not your typical Frenchman.

Two days before we left, he became convinced someone was stealing the oil he used on his salads. "I marked the level with a pencil this evening before I put it in the closet, so I'll have proof by tomorrow."

The next morning, when we were ready to take the bus back to Marrakech, Didier called Bill aside. "The bastards are definitely stealing it," he said. "There was only about an inch left…until I peed in it. I hope the damn thief enjoys his food today!"

We had only one night in Marrakech before our plane left for Paris. The Ali had no vacant rooms, so we checked into an adjacent hotel, where we met two young computer specialists—one from Greece, the other from Hong Kong. They had come solely to take the desert tour and had no intention of going out until the tour left the next morning. Like many others they felt there was something sinister about Morocco—too many strange odors, too many men on the street in relation to the women. They found the calls to prayer "eerie" and the ill-dressed beggars a threat. We tried to convince them their fear was unjustified and was stifling their appreciation of the country.

"No, all the men holding hands aren't gay," Bill assured them. "It's their custom—just a sign of friendship."

Bill offered to take them to the plaza and through the market.

"A Japanese girl told us it's dangerous in the *souks*," said Ling. "Someone snatched her billfold right out of her purse. She says it's almost impossible not to get lost. Do you know your way around, Bill?"

"I know my way around, but that doesn't mean I won't get lost. We always get lost, but someone will tell us how to get out," Bill tried to reassure them.

They still had reservations, but I don't think they liked the idea of sitting in their hotel room if two senior citizens were brave enough to go.

The four of us hadn't been in the plaza more than a couple of minutes when two of the ever-present hustlers approached. Their opening line was the usual: "Where are you from?"

Bill gave them his standard reply in Arabic: "I work here."

They were surprised and of course asked, "What do you do?"

"I work with the Moroccan police for the protection of tourists."

They made a cordial but rapid retreat.

Ling and I stopped to watch a tiny, barefoot fellow sitting cross-legged in the middle of the square. Why he had chosen that spot, we'd never know. In the midst of this noisy throng, he seemed oblivious to everything around him. Though his crossed eyes were three inches from a page of the Koran, he was probably repeating words he'd memorized.

I've often questioned the lack of eyeglasses in developing countries. Is there a dearth of oculists? Do pharmacies not sell simple ones for magnification? Perhaps it's a cultural bias.

The square intrigued Yannis, and he wanted to absorb it all. He was disappointed the fortune-tellers sitting under tiny umbrellas and whispering predictions didn't speak anything he could understand. He and Bill wandered over to examine the table of teeth the tooth puller had on display to advertise his prowess with pliers, while Ling went with me to the spice area. I asked one of the sellers, who sat on the ground surrounded by his saffron and the red, green, and yellow spice, for the spice used on kebabs. He filled a clear plastic sack with a red powder for me.

Bill steered us around a snake handler. He knew if tourists weren't wary, they'd likely find a snake around their neck and be forced to give the owner money to be released.

As we left the square and entered the *souk*, Yannis was walking with Bill; Ling held my arm, and I don't think it was for my protection. Unfortunately a group of kids began following us, chanting, "Bruce Lee, Bruce Lee." All the street urchins knew the martial arts champion, and they obviously thought Ling looked like him. This large entourage didn't allay his fear.

We had enough knowledge and persuasion to keep Yannis from buying the one-of-a-kind, fossilized, three-million-year-old ammonite he liked. It didn't pass the penknife test.

We spent considerable time in the apothecary shops so Yannis could buy the sticks of walnut root some Moroccans used to clean their teeth. The aphrodisiacs and the horns and talons that worked magic intrigued him. Ling was less captivated. I doubt he saw much that was different from Asian markets. I learned the red powder I'd bought for my kebabs would keep me headache free for a lifetime.

At least three of us had fun. We got e-mail and Christmas cards from Yannis for several years.

35

Turkey: "But You Said No Monuments!"

(Ina)

Bill said, "The directions are in that book," nodding to a *Guide Bleu* on the dashboard.

"This book is a 1950 edition! And besides, it's in Italian."

"The date doesn't matter, and aren't you aware that all roads lead to Rome?"

I didn't bother to comment that Rome wasn't our destination or that Turkey was somewhat farther along, like beyond Greece. Bill always drove the camper, and this was close enough for him. Besides, he liked asking people for directions; it gave him a chance to use a different language.

I suggested another gondola ride would be enjoyable, so he agreed to book a boat from Venice. Their service didn't begin until June so we drove to Ancona, a port in Southern Italy, where two old men motioned us aboard a battered ferry for our overnight trip to Greece. With the aid of Bill's *National Geographic* map of ancient Greece, we somehow found our way to Athens and through her dense traffic to her hectic port of Piraeus, where we caught another ferry to Samos—one of the few Greek islands that allowed a connection with Turkey.

In Samos a fellow helped Bill inflate the Russian raft he bought at the Free Market in Ukraine and invited us to their celebration of Orthodox Easter. Bill declined because early the next morning we were to sail for Turkey. I was glad. I learned the traditional meal served after midnight mass was tripe soup.

Many of those aboard our ferry were expat Europeans returning to Turkey from their three-month obligatory visa renewals. At the midway point in the Aegean Sea, one of the crew lowered the blue-and-white Greek flag. The Turkish star and crescent was pulled aloft amid exuberant clapping and cheering. Caps popped off bottles of beer. Drinking sparked more interaction, and we met Martin, a Dutch expat.

When we landed at Çe me, Martin waited for our van to clear customs. He said, "It's crucial to register it or you can't get it out of the country." He then directed us to a parking area in front of his house and invited us to join him and his friends for dinner.

Turkish cuisine, along with French and Chinese, ranks among the best in the world. On previous visits we had always enjoyed the Turkish invitation to "come look in our window," a waiter's summons to select from foods displayed in his refrigerated case. This time we deferred to our host.

As we sipped *raki*, an anise-flavored drink, the hors d'oeuvres began appearing: cucumbers, cauliflower, leeks, tomatoes—vegetables frittered or grilled, then served in yogurt sauce or flavored with a subtle mixture of spices. We scooped up these appetizers with flatbread. Next came a "swooning imam," a famous Turkish eggplant dish. After sampling it, I had no trouble solving the ongoing debate over why it had that name. True, the imam might have been shocked after learning how much his wife spent for the olive oil, but it was so delicious I felt sure it would have made even a religious leader swoon.

A swordfish in a hazelnut sauce followed. Then whether it was lamb in pastry, meatballs in tomato sauce, fried mussels, or chicken with walnuts, one of the thirteen people in attendance encouraged us to, "Try this!" And we did. We tasted it all.

With each new treat, we listened sympathetically to the indignities the Greeks had perpetrated in their long running dispute with Turkey over possession of Cyprus. The most recent allegation: the Greeks were floating their garbage over to pollute the Turkish beaches.

Even before dessert I was satiated, but still I managed a lady's navel, a pastry filled with pistachio. As we sat drinking our tiny cups of Turkish *kahve*, with a full moon dancing and reflecting off the Aegean Sea, I realized this was indeed an evening to savor.

The next day we drove to Izmir—ancient Smyrna—home of the poet Homer. When we stopped at its largest market, I wandered off to browse the prized Turkish rugs, while Bill went on a search for a dictionary. Atatürk, the renowned father of modern Turkey, had changed the nation's Arabic alphabet to Latin letters. But with all their diacritical marks, words still looked complicated.

Since Turkey is a member of NATO, Bill had learned a little of the language from his students. By the time he bought the "right" dictionary, I had moved on. He located me browsing among the copper candlesticks and brass pots. It was now late in the day, so we parked on a street by the port to spend the night.

Bill returned from his evening exploration with a big grin on his face. "Do I look wealthy or just handsome?"

"Hmm," I said. "Definitely handsome. Why? Were you propositioned?"

"I was. Twice! Both times by a good-looking guy."

From friends who had taught in Turkey, we knew homosexuality was frowned on, though these casual encounters didn't cause nearly as much trouble as having an illicit affair with a Turkish female.

The next morning over coffee, Bill said, "Let's go to Istanbul. There's no greater place to people watch."

"Yep, Istanbul is great. Remember how we laughed at the sign in our hotel: 'No making of rumors or dirting on the floor.' But since we're in our camper, I think we should stick to our original decision."

"But on our way, we could stop to see the Rutting Camel Wrestling Festival!"

"Oh, I do hate for you to miss that."

Negotiation ended after I promised I wouldn't insist on stopping to admire any of the many monuments we had seen before.

Ephesus was our first stop. It's one of the best-preserved ancient cities around the Mediterranean and the location of the Temple of Athena, one of the Seven Wonders of the Ancient World. Christians visit because Mary was here with the Apostle John, and some think she was buried nearby. And, after preaching that the images of Artemis were not divine, Saint Paul was imprisoned here.

"Bill, let's take a break." Before he could accuse me of breeching our agreement, I explained, "I don't want to revisit anything. What I wanted to see doesn't qualify as a monument. It's a recently restored Roman public toilet."

We located it in the ancient city next to the brothel. Along the four sides of this rectangular room were "thrones" sufficient for forty male bottoms.

On our way out, Bill bought ten postcards for friends of this unique gathering place of the Roman elite.

An hour or so later, when we arrived at Bodrum, I didn't suggest stopping to see the ancient site of Halicarnassus, another of the Seven Wonders of the Ancient World to see the most magnificent tomb in the world. I was on the lookout for a phone booth, eager to call Sally, a friend I had worked with at SHAPE.

For four summers Sally and Suat, her Turkish-born husband, came to live in a village outside Bodrum, where he supervised the building of their retirement home. The peasants in the small village expected Suat, a California architect, to possess a wide range of expertise. He had been asked to interpret the law and settle their disputes. They had granted him the privilege of selecting—and paying for—new curtains for the mayor's office. And each year Suat brought a supply of Alka-Seltzer —his neighbors believed the fizz worked magic on all ailments. So his most important function became dispensing doctor.

Suat had arrived with an elaborate set of blueprints that met California earthquake standards, but he had learned the Turks here had a different criterion. Earthquakes, they could ignore, but not roof tiles. Tiles must be red and identical to those of the other villagers so the houses would harmonize.

In Bodrum a local helped me make my phone call, and Sally invited us to their village across the bay.

Bill was cautious driving in rural Turkey. One of our friends who taught in Izmir had objected to the price he'd been charged for killing a goat that had strayed into his path on a mountain bend. The punch he'd received in the dispute broke his nose.

To avoid ducks and chickens, Bill drove slowly along the well-rutted road. He planned to stop and ask for directions, but when we got near Sally's house, he didn't get the chance. Four neighbors were out waving. They already knew who we were and what we were about, and were pointing the way to Sally's house.

Suat said he had sold their car after they moved here, preferring to get to Bodrum by boat; nevertheless, he had a slew of Turkish automobile stories.

"The first time we left here to go to the States," he told us, "though I questioned its roadworthiness, I called our local taxi. The owner assured me he could get us to the airport safely and on time. His headlights were dim, but he brought along a local boy who sprawled over the hood of the car and hung on to the hood ornament so he could shine a flashlight on the road. The taxi sped us through the night."

After a look at their new redesigned house and Sally's garden, we left a few hours later with some of her fresh tomatoes and eggs, and recommendations of places to visit.

How many times in Europe had we driven miles out of our way to visit the ruins of an older civilization? In Turkey the remains of the various cultures that had swept through Asia Minor were scattered all over—far too many for the government to keep them in presentable condition. As we bicycled around, I saw a few, but with my attention divided between history and patches of sand, I didn't always stay upright.

At Sally's suggestion we went to see a Greek amphitheater Alexander the Great had built. Bill hiked up the steps. I struggled up the first 150 before sinking down to admire it. He continued the climb and was obviously dreaming as he sat on one of the many curved stone seats higher up. The silence was serene until several "Hellllooo, Iiiinnaaaa"s came echoing off the mountain walls.

The next time, when he walked off to get a closer look at two tall Lydian statues guarding the entrance to some tombs, I chose to remain in the camper to study them with our binoculars. When he returned, I asked, "Why did I have to promise not to revisit monuments? This is the second time I've had to wait while you were out studying them."

"They're not monuments I've been looking at," he assured me.

"Oh?"

"They're ruins!"

"My most humble apologies. I'm sorry I failed to recognize that distinction, oh wise one!"

"Apologies accepted. I don't epect you to know everything!"

We spent most of our nights in small Aegean ports rather than in the campgrounds, which proudly advertised "everytime hot water!" The many solar panels we saw vouched for this truth—there are a reported three hundred days of sunshine per year here.

We thought the Turks were dignified but reserved until Bill made contact. I should rephrase that. The Turks are friendly. Bill rarely failed to make contact. His limited Turkish vocabulary opened doors. They got us an invitation to an open-air wedding reception. The bride wore a long, white wedding gown and the groom a black suit. I wondered if Turkish brides had traditionally worn white, or were they dressing as Westerners, as Atatürk had decreed?

I suggested we move along faster so we could visit another of our friends at the military base in Adana, but Bill liked dawdling.

We had an idyllic lifestyle by the glistening Aegean Sea—Bill swam, and I browsed through markets, where everything cost only a few *liras*. It was pleasing to be awakened by the call to prayer and see people either hurrying to the mosque or spreading their prayer rugs to pray on the streets or wherever they happened to be. I would have enjoyed shopping for food, but it was too much fun eating in their restaurants.

With June nearly over, it was getting hot, so it was time to head home.

Bill had read a detective story in the French magazine *GEO*. An English archeologist found a knife of black obsidian on the southern coast of Turkey. There was no obsidian in this area, so he excavated where some was reported to be in the north. In Çatalhöyük by a mound near a fork of two rivers, he uncovered one of the world's oldest city maps. The people who lived there had used holes in the tops of their dome-shaped homes as the entrances. Inside were mirrors, eating utensils, and makeup implements, but the fresco map was the most important find. Bill wanted to see it, so he stopped at a tourist agency for directions.

The manager had once lived in Belgium and became excited over the opportunity to speak French, so we spent the afternoon with him. He plied us with posters, maps, apple tea, and assurances that there was little to see at the fork, so we opted for his recommendation to go to the world's most famous hot springs. Hammans, similar to Roman baths, are features throughout Turkey, and I looked forward to bathing in this most famous UNESCO World Heritage site.

The inland route to Pamukkale was both long and dusty, but when we arrived, the site was spectacular. Cascading water had cut through various levels of the glistening white limestone to form cotton castles, the name given to these steaming pools. Bathing there was no longer allowed—the castles had become too fragile.

When we got to town, I grabbed my bathing suit and towel, ready to head for one of the town's many spas.

"If we go to a spa, we'll have to get a key, take a shower, and go through a lot of rigmarole," Bill said while changing clothes in the back of the van. "We passed several places. If they're good enough for the Turks to bathe in, they're good enough for us."

I grumbled and thought about going alone, but instead changed clothes and followed him to a ditch where the hot water arrives before it's piped into the spas. We plopped in beside a half-dozen colorful individuals who were clearly surprised when we joined them, though one tough-looking male gave me a gold-toothed smile. Bill immediately tried his Turkish, but realized they spoke a mixture of bastard Romance languages. Then he turned to me and said, "They're travelers too."

By that time I was well aware we had joined a band of Gypsies.

Bathing in the ditch was so refreshing I hated to get out. That night, after another wonderful meal, it was easy to fall asleep in a big parking lot, especially when the nightingales began to sing.

The next morning I realized my evening serenade hadn't been the real thing. The songs had come from pink clay whistles filled with water. We bought a dozen from the young boys who sold them for ten cents each. We, along with our neighbors, could now join our two resident nightingales in Port Marly on summer evenings.

Before we left Turkey, Bill wanted one last early-morning bike ride. He said he was pedaling along but stopped abruptly when he heard screaming—what sounded like someone being murdered. Instead, he witnessed the birth of a camel. After the owner cut the umbilical cord, he began mouth-to-mouth resuscitation to keep from losing his newborn treasure. Bill, in his role of observing midwife helped rope off a space to keep the crowds back and stayed until he was satisfied the baby would survive.

It seemed a shame to retrace our route home, so we detoured by the island of Rhodes. Again we spent our nights facing the port, this time at the foot of the ancient city wall. Bill lingered during his morning swim to examine the pink granite columns that lay just below the surface.

In the afternoons we absorbed more history while roaming the grounds of a castle owned by the monks and knights who had supported the crusaders. After the Muslims had regained control of Jerusalem, the Knights Templar had relocated here, where they became known as the Knights of Rhodes.

In preparation for our return through Greece, I tried reading aloud from the *National Geographic* map about the nearby sights of ancient Greece. But as usual, once Bill's homing instincts blossom, he doesn't dally.

The sign "Gulah, gulah" is often posted at the exit of a Turkish village. It translates "Go with smiles." This vagabonding experience elicited big smiles from both of us.

With more than ten thousand years of continuous civilization, I thought Turkish monuments were incomparable. Their numerous ruins fascinated Bill.

36

PERU: WE "BLAZE" AN INCA TRAIL

(Ina)

It was 2:00 a.m. by the time we got into Lima. Even with our taxi driver's relentless pounding, it took some time for the sleepy clerk to unbolt the hotel's heavy wooden door. Even before it was fully open, Bill gave me a gentle push, propelling me in, while saying to the night clerk, "No, we don't have a reservation."

We followed the fellow's weary shuffle. He mumbled something, and handed us a key before sliding back onto the cot behind the desk.

"See?" said Bill. "I told you we wouldn't have trouble getting a room."

"A brilliant maneuver," I mumbled, dragging my backpack up the steps.

I came looking forward to not only seeing Machu Picchu, but also the other Andean scenery, so during our late breakfast, I steered the conversation to altitude sickness. "Bill, it's the rapid change that causes most people to suffer from *el soroche*. But if we go to Cusco by bus rather than fly, we will make several overnight stops. That would give our bodies time to adjust to the height before we get to Machu Picchu."

Bill acquiesced and bought our bus tickets before we made our way up the walking street that led to Lima's main square. The square dates from the 1500s, the time Francisco Pizarro and his Spanish conquistadors conquered the Incas. Nearby was their Inquisition Museum. We learned it contained the same racks and water-torture instruments as the one we'd visited in Madrid. But, according to this guide, "More than two thousand Jews and Muslims were burned for heresy in Spain while here in my country, that happened to only a handful of priests." He failed to mention that those priests had been caught cohabiting with native women. Neither did he say Indians were excluded from the Inquisition because they were considered "not fully rational." But as we left, he stated, for at least the third time, that his church vehemently opposed the shedding of blood.

And Bill assured him that was "indeed a Christian attitude."

I then led us across the street to visit Parliament, but the guard informed us it was in recess, so I suggested we follow a sign that pointed to China Town. Instead of the long, dark alleys and intriguing hallways we expected, there was one short, modern street with a combination hardware/trinket store and two restaurants.

Bill decided he should take over guide duty. Our next destination wouldn't have been on my list of places, as it was Lima's equivalent of the Bronx. To get there we walked behind the presidential palace to look over the two armored tanks blocking the street. They were positioned to head off demonstrations against President Fujimori's upcoming reelection tactics. We then came to a river, whose Indian name translated as "the river that speaks." It spoke all right. Its odor rivaled the leather-tanning *souks* in Morocco. A thick, green slime held stationary the rotting garbage thrown into its sluggish water.

Before crossing the bridge, Bill repeated the instructions he frequently gave me: "If people think you belong, nobody will bother you, so relax and walk as though you're not looking at anyone or anything."

His logic made as much sense as biting into a sandwich I knew contained a razor blade, but I admit we have never been mugged in all the seedy areas he has dragged me through. In the growing darkness, we sauntered past persistent hawkers selling rusty locks, old clothes, plastic buckets, and single cigarettes. And though I wasn't looking at anyone or anything, it was obvious there was a bar on every corner, and ragged, grimy-faced kids were grabbing my sleeves and begging for money. Everything I wasn't looking at spoke of abject poverty.

I had no appetite at dinner. Though my mind told me the fish on my plate hadn't come from that polluted water—nothing could live in it—I had difficulty swallowing. While Bill attacked his food with his usual enjoyment, I read the following in our guidebook: "It is not safe to cross the Rimac River even during daylight hours, for like many poverty-stricken…"

Bill dismissed my reading. "That guidebook was written for people who only feel safe behind the fence of a Club Med. We don't travel like that."

It was hard, but I refrained from replying.

On the second morning, we took a bus to some pre-Inca ruins outside Lima. Bill began translating salient facts from a brochure I picked up at the entrance. "This was one of their most important oracle sites…Major decisions were never made without consulting the will of the gods…The earth's creator and the sun were worshipped here."

I put my hand over his mouth and pointed to this sign:

PACACAMA TEMPLE
900–1533 AC
Wari-Ishmay Culture

Arriving to the town we began to walk straight to La Mezquita a great site in the sanctuary. In the first gate we found two gatekeepers who we asked them to let us see and talk to Pachacama and they said that nobody could see him before to talk to the priest, Hernando Pizarro said they came from spain, avery for peace, and needed to see him anyway and so against their consent, they got there up. The Mezquita (Huaca) crossing many doors before which had three entries in spiral way, Miguel de Estete, 1533

Not Entance

"If all their signs are as enlightening as this one, I won't need your translation."

The following morning our driver sped through the early morning traffic, not pausing at the red lights. At the entrance to a one-way street, he slammed on his brakes and spun his taxi around before speeding for a block and a half in reverse. After screeching to a halt, he leaped out, opened my door, and with a flourish gestured toward the entrance to Lima's newly opened bus station.

Our Cruz del Sur bus had reclining seats, a clean toilet, and an attentive hostess, who served us refreshments and box lunches. While a *Miami Vice* video played on the TV screen in front, I enjoyed the view out the window. Yellow broom dotted with bright flowers mingled with the red earth to form natural abstract paintings. When I saw cacti planted on the tops of the walls to deter intruders, I thought it had much more aesthetic appeal than the broken pieces of glass cemented in other places. I became adept at distinguishing llamas from alpacas. We weren't often close enough to identify an alpaca by its long eyelashes, but I soon realized the llama's tail sticks up differently. The Incan saying "God gave the Indians the llama because he knew they were poor" made sense—they were the ones carrying the heavy loads.

We climbed more than ten thousand feet before our bus made the first stopover in Huyancayo on market day. Indian women, who were either smoking cigars or chewing coca leaves, held up their alpaca sweaters and blankets. All of them wore hats. Some were tunnel-shaped with dangling ear coverings, made from multi-colored alpaca wool. Others resembled men's hats, but with wider brims turned slightly upward. We walked around, pulling the sweet cotton-candy fluff out of catalpa-like beans, and enjoyed our day as much as the regiment of flies that covered the meat hanging in the stalls.

The next morning we watched the gourd engraving that had made this area famous. I hadn't realized the designs weren't inked on until we were shown how cuts were made with tools similar to the ones used on leather. A burnishing stick applied to the cuts created the contrasting colors. Bill bought a signed gourd from a well-known engraver who had spent more than a year carving it. Though it was only the size of a small pear, the artist had etched more than a hundred plants, animals, and buildings along with farmers and their tools.

Bill wasn't at all happy to learn first-class buses didn't continue to Cusco. Due to poor road conditions, only local buses made the run. He also learned that Peruvians carry their stoves and cooking utensils, as well as small livestock with them when they travel. Not only were we crowded; the bus exuded a variety of odors. Our driver demonstrated two South American driving truths: #1 All driver have the right of way. #2 If you don't give it to him, there is room for both.

In my effort to spark a bit of enthusiasm, I related the Incas' creation myth. "Cusco is considered the navel of the earth. During the hundred years of their empire, the Incas built roads stretching from Chile all the way to Colombia to link up their distant provinces with Cusco."

Bill's unimpressed reply: "And were you also aware when you chose this route these original roads had never been improved?"

The bus's nonexistent shock absorbers did maximize the road's irregularities, but I found the trip quite...colorful.

"I'm going to pretend I'm not inside the drum of a cement mixer and meditate," Bill said. He wrapped his partial in a handkerchief and put it in his shirt pocket—it bounced against the armrest a number of times before it broke.

We finally arrived in Ayacucho, which means in Quechua, the language of the Incas, "OK, let's stop here."

"We're not halfway to Cusco," Bill announced, "but I have had more than enough of your 'experiencing Andean scenery from a bus.' I'm taking a plane."

I quietly accompanied him to buy tickets.

As we strolled around the town known as the hotbed of political activity for the Sendero Luminoso (Shining Path) Communist Party, I realized something didn't feel right. When I returned from my restroom inspection, Bill asked, "What in the world's the matter? You look like someone tried to rape you."

I confessed that my credit cards were no longer nestled safely in my bra—where I carry them when we travel. We rushed back to the airline office. After an assurance we had not left them there, we located the police station. They advised us to cancel them. Since I was confident I hadn't been "bra napped," we opted for a half gamble and withdrew the maximum allowed, which wasn't a lot, from an ATM machine with Bill's card, then canceled them. Little seemed worse than being stranded in South America without money, but we still had one card with Bill's picture. I contacted my sister and arranged for her to send another card to me at the American Express office in La Paz.

37

Peru: Machu Picchu

(Ina)

On our flight to Cusco, Bill raved about the beauty of the Andean scenery from his "vantage point in the sky." I quietly drank my Incan cola—a greenish-yellow drink made from local fruits that delivered a mainline shot of dextrose.

My priority was a trip to the lost city of the Incas. The Incas considered walking the Inca Trail to Machu Picchu an act of devotion. My preference would have been to join an organized hike along the trail, with my arrival timed to coincide with the sun god peeping over the mountain. But for me, the only realistic choice was getting on one of the trains from Cusco that zigzagged up the mountain because of the steep incline.

"Our option," I told Bill, "is between riding in a luxury car while dining and drinking a pisco sour, or taking the first-class train."

Bill bought tickets for a third option.

While we sat on the local train's wooden bench, he conversed with two Carmelite nuns from Bolivia who would only have a few hours at Machu Picchu—they were required to return to Cusco to spend the night at the convent. They showed him their clandestine key chains, admitting Mother Superior wouldn't like it if she knew they had spent money on something so frivolous. "But we wanted souvenirs of our vacation," they confided, giggling like schoolgirls. "And this is all we could afford."

At their mission, the nuns slept in an open field in freezing weather during the week so they could teach the tin miners' children. Disease was rampant, as the miners and their families bathed and drank water from a polluted river. Surely if Mother Superior discovered their ten-cent key chains, she'd realize they had already done enough penance.

Our train arrived at Aguas Calientes, the closest town, only an hour late. We found a hotel and caught a bus up to Machu Picchu. I proposed we walk back up the Inca Trail far enough so we could at least look down on the site. I forgot Peru is in the tropics; at six o'clock the sun sets. The site closed at five so we were too late to begin our visit.

Bill pointed to a sign: "A thirty-minute walk to Aguas Calientes." Instead of waiting for the bus to take us back we opted for that, assuming it would take us about twice as long.

Teams of young Indian boys in costume who were participating in this interschool race kept running past us. The thought of soaking in one of the thermal baths in the town kept me making my way down the endless steps.

The baths close at sunset. We arrived after dark. Though most walkers took less than the almost three hours we clocked, they too felt duped by that sign.

Bill assisted me to the nearest restaurant where we sat outside under a full moon, listening to the haunting Andean panpipe melodies. It was magical. In Paris, when I heard Peruvian entertainers, they became pied pipers I wanted to follow wherever they led. Here I listened quietly, trying not to move my sore muscles.

The next day, though my legs proved even less cooperative, we visited various temples, tombs, and fountains. At the Hitching Post of the Sun, where the sun god first appears, we sat while at least five tour groups passed, intrigued by the conflicting stories surrounding this astro-agricultural clock. No one gave the same information.

Two groups stood with outstretched arms and fingers, seeking to absorb the mystical rays their guide said the clock radiated.

I left with my own unique collection of Inca lore. I selected the stories I liked best. As the Incas never developed a system of writing, their history couldn't be confirmed, and mine can't be refuted.

No words or photos can do Machu Picchu justice. Being there is an unbelievable experience I wish everyone could have.

The local train took us back to Cusco, where Bill found us a room before he headed to their busy main square. Throughout the day, tour groups shuffled in and out of the baroque, seventeenth-century cathedral that occupies one side of the square. Young people frequent the Mama Africa club, and two Internet cafés do a brisk business, so a park bench became Bill's cultural-exchange headquarters.

When any tourist sat on one of the benches, kids came running to ask, "Where are you from?" Bill's answer sent them quoting: "Capital: Washington, DC. Three branches of government: executive, judicial, legislative: Chief exports…" They never missed a beat. How often their information was updated, how many countries they covered, or who was responsible for their learning, we didn't know. But their spiel was the introduction they needed to sell postcards or give shoeshines.

Bill often told me he couldn't remember a place where he'd spent several days with his language exchange sign without meeting at least one memorable character. Francisco was no exception. He was a fiftyish dandy, with graying sideburns, brown hair and brown eyes and had a "been everywhere, done everything" look. Francisco said he'd married five times and had fathered fourteen children. Bill guessed his primary occupation was still gigolo. He claimed fluency in seven languages, but after a brief exchange in Italian, which scarcely exceeded "*buongiorno,*" he switched back to Spanish.

"I was making it big in Cologne, Germany—had four kids, a good salary, big car—but I couldn't stand my wife's bourgeois attitude and her small-minded friends, so I took off." Without a pause, Francisco continued, "Do you know Venice, California?"

"Yes, very well," Bill answered.

"Lived there for a year and was in several movies. But you need the right connections to make it big in Hollywood."

"Why did you go to the States?"

"To see one of my daughters. My first wife was from Lima. She took her to the States when she was a year old. My daughter wanted to see me so bad, she sent me a ticket for Los Angeles. Like I said, if you don't have connections in Hollywood, you're not going to make it. My first wife didn't want me around, so she tried to fuck up my visa. That's why I joined the army. I was sworn in, and they sent me to Fort Dix, New Jersey. But after three weeks, the doctors insisted I had a lung problem. I got forced out on a medical discharge with five dollars more than the cost of a ticket back to Lima. I'd had enough of the States. I'm attached to my homeland, so I came back, though life here isn't easy."

Bill said he figured the next phrase was going to be a request for money, but Francisco pulled out a letter and asked him to check it. It was a threat of legal actions against the US Army.

"The authorities at Fort Mead, the base where they keep all army records, insist they can't find my medical discharge. They damn well know I deserve a disability pension, but they don't want to give it to me, so they say I don't exist."

Bill made corrections and wished Francisco good luck.

Our visitors' tickets for the sights around Cusco were valid for two weeks. It took almost that long to get Bill to make the rounds, though he insisted on a second trip to the cathedral. During our first visit, we failed to notice a large painting that sparked interest. A local artist's depiction of the Last Supper portrayed the disciples dining on Peru's national dish: the guinea pig.

To tease me Bill asked one of his regular exchangers—the one who reported on which restaurant had the best menu that day—to give me his recipe for roasting this gourmet delight. The fellow got so excited that part of his explanation was in Spanish.

When Bill questioned me, I said, "Oh, he even wrote down all the spices. I'm on my way to pick them up so I can make this for

Bertile and Emmanuelle. I'll tell them it's doubly authentic because before you killed it, I did what the Indians do: I passed it along your body so it would absorb all of your diseases. Don't you think that should make us all enjoy it more?"

Bill took a day tour with me through the Sacred Valley, the route that leads up to Machu Picchu. I thought some of their much-touted coca-leaf tea might alleviate some of the effects of the altitude, but it didn't solve my aging problem. I couldn't climb the steep steps at the brisk pace set by our guide and the under-thirty set we were with. I saw the terraced hillsides and irrigation systems from a distance, but I learned the Incas had kept their mathematical records with a *quipu* (knot), and with strings of various colors and lengths. Their huge stone constructions were so exact, they fit together as well as the Egyptian pyramids.

When Bill decided it was time to leave Peru, I told him our choice for getting to Puno was between the train and the bus. He checked the guidebook and we took the train.

On arrival in Puno, we went to an agency to book onward travel to Bolivia but were told, "The rules have changed," the agent said. "You can't get visas at the border anymore. You must get them from the consulate here."

On our way to the consulate, we walked through a flea market. It took effort to pull Bill away from a stall where they were selling antique knives. A block farther along, we saw a plaque for the consulate on an apartment building and climbed to the second floor only to learn their business hours were Monday through Friday. It was Saturday. Having no desire to stay in Puno, Bill rang the doorbell. The consul appeared wearing pajamas, a maroon robe, and a disgruntled expression. Bill waved our passports—with a five dollar bill covering six ones. Feigning ignorance of the language, he said, "Please, senor, *grande problema*. Amigos in Copacabana. No possible wait."

The consul saw the money and the passports and made a negative movement of his head, but he didn't close the door. Instead he rubbed his thumbs against the tips of his fingers, frowned, and said, "Better you wait till Monday. Much expensive."

"But amigos worry. Can't wait."

The consul led us into a waiting room, went into his office. He came out with an official-looking notebook. "Maybe," he said, "you pay twenty dollars?"

Bill nodded an affirmative.

He left again, mumbling, "Maybe say no." Then from his office came, "*Hola*, La Paz." This was followed by several loud repetitions of "*Problema. Permisione. Problema*"—to what Bill thought was a non-existent second party.

The consul came back with a big smile. "*Bueno, bueno.* You lucky but must pay twenty-five dollars."

Bill paid him the twenty-five plus the price of our visas.

When we left, Bill said, "I would have gone up to thirty-five. If we had waited until Monday, he'd have worked out some other imaginary tax anyway.

38

Bolivia: Our Hotel near the Witches' Market

(Ina)

The squalid adobe huts of the Aymara Indians were our introduction to La Paz. In other locations a mountain view is the prime real estate, but in Bolivia wealthy inhabitants shun the heights of El Alto to opt for valley living. A difference of three thousand-plus feet makes for easier breathing if you're already nearly two miles above sea level.

Our hotel was located in the center but still a two-block, dig-in-your-toes drop to the Plaza San Francisco. While Bill set up his language sign, I walked around the plaza to check out the bowler hats the Aymara women wore. One story from the '20s says a Bolivian outfitter accidentally ordered too many derby hats, so he marketed his surplus as women's wear. The style caught on, as the women believed the hats enhanced fertility. They still wear sizes Westerners think are too small for their heads.

When I returned from my tour, Bill waved me over and introduced me to two of his jeans-and-sport-shirted students. "They're policemen," he explained. "They say we shouldn't come here after dark. This is where thieves who know all the tricks sleep."

The taller of the two said, "If you walk around alone, someone is going to spray your jacket with a greenish goop. He'll point to the sky and shout, 'Paloma.' While he's helping you clean off the 'pigeon shit,' his partner will disappear with your backpack."

Being forewarned, I assumed I'd be safe, but within the hour, while sitting on a low wall watching the gestures of the storytellers, I felt a plop hit the shoulder of my jacket. A young man came waving his handkerchief. I turned and saw his partner approaching from behind.

I clutched my pack against my chest and said, "You can't pull that on me! I know you're a thief."

He laughed and went in search of someone less informed.

With my roll of pink toilet paper, I tried cleaning off the mess. Kleenex is both expensive and hard to find, so like most travelers, I carried a roll of toilet paper for the constant nasal drip caused by the cold, humid climate. I used what was left, but an ugly stain remained. The name La Paz refers to the City of Our Lady of Peace. She wasn't living up to her name—peaceful was not how I felt.

The throng around Plaza San Francisco was in constant motion. Most were either illiterate Indians or poor working people too busy surviving to stop for lessons. Bill stayed just long enough to watch the hawkers of fake antiques and fossils and to check with the policemen whether he was correct about those he thought were pickpockets.

He learned the central courthouse was only two blocks up a hill, so we went to their main courtroom. He asked the guard if there were any trials in session we could visit.

"Yes," the guard said. "Go up to any of the floors and choose."

We entered a chamber on the third floor, where a lawyer was whispering advice to a female with a black eye. She had multiple bruises, and a white patch covered her left ear.

When the judge walked in, everyone stood. He banged his gavel. Everyone sat except the defense lawyer. The judge nodded for him to begin.

"Senor Gomez is too ill to appear. He swears he will never lose his temper again."

The judge ran his finger down the dossier. "That's the same promise he made after his five previous arrests. This time the accused will spend one year in prison."

I could understand some of what was going on—enough to realize their "justice" was quick. Bill learned later this isn't always the case.

The following day we went to another plaza, this one bordered on one side by the parliament and on another side by the presidential palace. Not long after we sat down on a bench to watch the activity, a man approached. "I'm desperate," he pleaded. "My mother is in the hospital, but she's dying because the government won't spend ten dollars for the medicine to save her."

"That's terrible," Bill sympathized. "Let's go call. I'll ask for the name of the medicine."

The man grumbled before throwing his arms in the air and storming off.

Hustling is rampant. Bolivia is one of the poorest countries in South America. The poverty Simon Bolivar found when he liberated the country from Spain still exists.

We didn't linger at this plaza either—there were more pigeons than people, but the moment Bill discovered Saint Andrews, Bolivia's largest university, he felt at home. He unrolled his sign by a stairway near an imposing, two-story painting of Che Guevara on the university's wall. Guevara died in Bolivia and is revered there.

On his third day at Saint Andrew's, Bill was invited to join an English class. Many students hoped to work as guides—one of the better-paying jobs. Yet when he asked how many of them had traveled to other countries, only one girl raised her hand—her mother was from Brazil.

I work hard not to get pulled into Bill's language exchanges, though this time I enjoyed helping one student with her assignment. It dealt with what's expected if someone from another nationality invites you to dinner. Their book gave these tips: North Americans will expect you to arrive on time…You have several hours' leeway with the French…With the Italians even more…In some South American countries, it is possible to show up the next day and still be welcomed.

It didn't take long before I'd seen enough squalor on my walks. I suggested we take a bus to visit a suburb. La Paz's bus system is user friendly. Their minibuses will stop anywhere. Major destinations are displayed either by a sign on top or on the windshield of the bus. A voice also calls out the route for the sight impaired or illiterates. The downside: it's not unusual for a twentieth person to squeeze into a fifteen-seater.

We passed the polluted Choqueyapu River, referred to by the locals as Choke River. It runs underground through most of the city center, but on the outskirts it's quite easy to see and much easier to smell.

High walls obscure most of the houses in the suburbs. We thought it likely the most prosperous-looking manor belonged to a government official. When Bill asked the uniformed guard—there is usually a guard at the entrance gate to these houses—he answered proudly, "This is the home of the president of the Bolivian football team!" We should have remembered football's importance in South America.

After a third week, I strongly suggested it was time to move along. Bill agreed and proposed we join the other daredevils who traveled to Coroico, down what was deemed "the world's most dangerous road."

"But Bill," I protested, "every other week at least one vehicle goes over the edge on the way there."

"Minivans, the type we'll take, don't have a problem," he said. "The young people like going down it on dirt bikes, but I don't think you would like that."

"You know me well, don't you?"

Before we went, I suggested we at least buy one of the good-luck amulets from the witches' market next to our hotel. We looked, but left empty handed. A dried llama fetus was suggested as the most effective item for this venture. I shouldn't have worried about added protection. A picture of Christ on the cross, mounted inside a horseshoe, hung from the rearview mirror of our van—the mini type that "doesn't normally have problems." A pink plastic statue of the Virgin Mary rested on the dashboard. She was draped with rosary beads that swung each time we hit a hole in the road. And before descending the most dangerous stretch—a steep, narrow, unpaved one-lane section that plunged about twelve thousand feet in fewer than forty miles—our driver got out, made the sign of the cross, and poured *chico*, the local brew, on the front tires. This potent, fermented offering is made from corn that has been steamed—after the kernels are thoroughly chewed to impregnate them with saliva. Chico was a gift to Mother Earth.

On our descent, the weather became warmer and the air easier to breathe. As uphill traffic always hugs the cliff side, we once had to back up fifty yards. Our driver had to find a spot wide enough for a truck to pass. Bill never failed to point out the crumbled carcasses of recent crashes. I looked at the oranges and the bunches of bananas ready for picking, and tried to focus on the trees that were so lush and thick they were like overgrown stalks of broccoli.

The Esmerelda Hotel overlooked a beautiful valley, and its food was a welcome change from the potatoes and rice we had eaten most days in La Paz. Bill proposed we walk through a tropical forest to a nearby waterfall. I read the posted warnings about the danger of going there, so my counter proposal was, "Let's accept the invitation from your student." The fellow lived in a neighboring town and had invited us to meet his wife, one of the many descendants of the black former slaves who lived in the area.

Before we did either, a heavy fog rolled in. The natives said fogs hung around for at least a week. I was all for waiting it out, but since we had already been there five days, Bill had met all the town's characters. "La Paz," he insisted, "has far more to offer."

"To whom?"

The normal three-hour return took five; a landslide blocked the road. At least in fog, overturned vehicles weren't easily seen. I was profoundly relieved to arrive safely in the slums of El Alto.

As we descended from there, I admitted La Paz shone like a crown of multicolored jewels, a magical welcome.

Near the center of town, Bill saw a billboard advertising a dental clinic. Early the next morning, we took a mini bus there to see about getting his partial repaired.

"No, it can't be fixed," the dentist told him. "I can make a replacement, but that's very expensive—sixty dollars!"

The dental chair wasn't the newest model, but the dentist followed a few normal procedures. On the day of the fitting, he didn't bother putting on his smock until the grinding got a bit tricky.

On the way back to our hotel, Bill tried getting my agreement that La Paz was simply wonderful.

"I haven't found it so wonderful," I said. "You're just excited about your dentist-without-a-smock deal. I hope you don't have a sore throat by morning."

39

BOLIVIA: LA PAZ'S MOST BIZARRE PRISON

(Bill)

I PERSUADED ONE of the girls in the hotel to tell Ina about her fascinating visit to San Pedro Prison. My plan didn't work. Ina's reply: "Of course she'd think a visit to any prison would be unique. She hasn't been dragged to as many as I have."

So the next day, I went by myself. I followed the advice the plainclothes detective had given me on the first day in Plaza San Francisco; I asked to see James, an African who had lived in London. A messenger brought him to the entrance, and James took me up to his room. While making coffee he told me, "Americans are lucky if they make it through the night here because of the money your government spends to eradicate poppy fields. The only people hated more are child molesters."

Then he said: "My first week here, all the prisoners were in the courtyard, watching television when we learned a man who had raped three young girls was arriving the next day. When the guards shoved the rapist into the courtyard, a dozen hairy arms grabbed him.

They punched him till blood flowed from his nose, ears, and mouth. Then they dragged him over to the pool in the middle of the courtyard and threw him into water they had fitted with electrodes. He shrieked and quivered in the electrified water while they jeered and clapped themselves into frenzy.

"Guards seldom come into the courtyard. They let prisoners settle things themselves.

"When he struggled to climb out, he got kicked in the face. As he lay bleeding in a corner of the pool, the electricity was turned off so they could yank him out. They slammed his skull on the cement edge. His brains spilled into the water."

I didn't relate his story to Ina or tell her James had said that for three days he couldn't eat the scraps of slop they served as food—it looked like the brain floating on the water. Instead, I suggested we spend the night there. "It just costs ten dollars. James said tourists stay there for the experience. One German girl lived with him for three months."

Ina gave a "nose squeezed in a vice" expression. "I'm not looking for that kind of thrill."

"San Pedro isn't like any prison I've taken you to," I continued. "James has a room with a kitchen all to himself. He paid the equivalent of three thousand US dollars for it. The wife of Rodrigo, his Colombian friend, was frying a tempting-smelling, garlicky dish when I visited them. She lives there with their two boys. They have a bathroom, so it costs five thousand. Money rules here."

I could see I was arousing her curiosity, so I continued.

"The cocaine king lives in a penthouse. He hired an architectural firm to build it on top of the prison. It has a sauna."

The next visiting day, the moment Ina and I walked through the gate, prisoners leaped on the courtyard's metal wire fence. Holding on with one hand, they pointed fingers at their chests while screaming, "James, I go!" On my first visit, I had given the messenger a hundred centavos—ten cents was big money to the poor souls at the bottom of the economic scale.

James was alerted, so he cleared the others out of the way to open a path for Ina. We took refuge in his room in the section named Alamo. When he went to his tiny kitchen to make tea, Ina looked over the more than fifty books on the two shelves above his color TV. Titles included *The Kama Sutra*, *Don Quixote*, and *Bolivian Penal Law*.

After tea James took us on a tour. "Prisoners who don't have money to buy rooms have to spend their nights here in the corridors on a this cold, cement floor."

I looked away when I saw the pool where the child molester had his brains bashed out.

Adjoining the courtyard was what looked like a small village. "Prisoners own the café, the grocery store, and the barbershop. One of my friends runs the billiard parlor."

Some prisoners were washing clothes. Water from their laundry dripped from the balcony where clothes were hanging.

We sat on the benches, and James introduced us to a friend Jorge who asked if we would be visiting Coroico. When I said we had been there, he asked if we'd mail a message to the owner of the Esmeralda Hotel. I agreed, so he hurried off to write it.

Ina said she didn't feel particularly uncomfortable, but one visit was enough. "I hate thinking about what life must be like for the prisoners' kids we saw riding bikes in the courtyard."

On my third visit, I brought some antibiotics. James said, "Medicine is pure gold." We took the penicillin to a young Italian who was in bad shape. Without funds he had little hope of ever seeing a doctor and no hope of getting medicine.

On this trip I learned almost everything is permitted in San Pedro for those with thick wallets. "If a prisoner wants a night on the town, he pays a hundred dollars plus the fee for a guard to accompany him," James told me.

The most lucrative racket is their "secret" cocaine lab. Twenty-liter cans of chemicals pass through the front gate like the Invisible Man. One morning, as I sat in James's room, I saw three people waiting for their fix outside his neighbor's door.

James said he had already served his four years. "I was due for release three months ago, but I have to wait until another judge is appointed so my papers can be signed by a quorum."

San Pedro Prison is so bizarre that Kafka couldn't describe all its folly. But so are the strange twists in the Bolivian justice system.

40

South America on His Own

(Ina)

"Are you sure you don't mind?" Bill asked for about the fourth time.

"Yes, Bill, I'm sure. I'm quite capable of getting to the airport in Lima by myself."

My original plan had both of us returning to Lima by the coastal route. I planned for us to visit sites along the way. From Lima I would fly to Texas, while Bill spent a month in Brazil. But he changed his mind and decided he'd prefer having more time in La Paz.

My month-long Bolivian visa was expiring. I'd either have to renew it or leave. The extra days in Peru appealed more than staying here since it would be my chance to see sights I had missed.

We agreed to e-mail whenever possible, and Bill said he'd call on Sunday mornings after I got to my sister's house. The trepidation I felt when I boarded an early-morning bus for my return to Lake Titicaca wasn't for me, but for Bill's well-being. I knew he would be off to the slums of El Alto as soon as I was out of sight. He hadn't been there. I assumed its lure was what was keeping him in La Paz.

My e-mail from Puno: Haven't encountered any major problems. Young people must be fond of their grandmothers because they were solicitous when I visited the floating islands from a reed boat and visited some more pre-Inca sites.

Bill's e-mail: I learned about a fascinating Indian fire ceremony in El Alto.

I didn't know what that might mean, but at least I knew he was still alive. When I got to Cusco, I thought it best not to mention that a llama had wandered onto the train track, and the delay had caused us to arrive in Cusco at night. Tourists were being advised not to be on the street after dark because the current popular method of robbery was to choke victims until they lost consciousness and then strip them of their clothes to delay the reporting.

I had looked over my fellow passengers and asked a kindly looking man with a husky son if I could share their taxi into town. Since it was now the high season, Cusco was packed. These friendly Dutch even helped me find a room.

My e-mail to Bill: Cusco is having a religious celebration. All the statues have been taken from the cathedrals and paraded around the square. Great fun. Glad I didn't miss it. Flying into Lima tomorrow.

Bill's e-mail to me: You would be proud of me. For several nights I've been attending church.

I interpreted this to mean he'd heard frenzied singing and had gone to join in.

Communicating from third world countries is iffy at best. Finding a place to send e-mails was hard enough; using their computers was even harder. Instead of a phone call in Texas, a letter arrived telling me about his El Alto night:

> Drunks—most of them Indians—staggered along, some in the middle of the street. They had no trouble spotting me, the senseless gringo who had ventured here alone. I considered leaving after they tried to grab my arm twice, but instead I took refuge in an eatery, where I ordered chicken soup. I figured boiling rendered cockroach droppings nontoxic.

After watching through the window, I realized arm grabbing was not reserved for gringos but was a harmless attempt either to talk or to mooch a drink.

The bar I went to afterward was down a dark hallway. A working girl approached me, but I told her I had AIDS and since I couldn't afford medicine, I was drinking away my last money. She insisted on buying me a second beer, and the boss at the cash register refused to let me pay for the first one.

On leaving I was halfway down the hallway when an Indian threw a match, and flames shot up, blocking the exit. I ran back inside the bar to look for another way out. There wasn't one! I raced back, determined to run through the fire, but the same guy was now stamping out the flames.

Back on the street, a drunken Indian grabbed me. I was so happy to still be alive I was returning his hug when I saw flames shoot up in the doorway of the next bar. I recognized the same Indian with a can of spray in his hand. He began stomping out his fire again. I never learned whether this was the fetish of a loose nut or an offering to the saint who watches over dens of iniquity.

I shuddered to think of what could have happened in El Alto to the "loose nut" dear to me. How like Bill to conjure up some mythical Indian fire ceremony!

In another bar with a door at the sidewalk, I attempted to convince a well-used female hostess that I wanted to watch the chanting, circle dancing, and clapping. But she shouted loud enough to be heard across the hullabaloo, "This gringo's from France." I was pulled into the circle.

Festivities were still going strong at five in the morning, when I felt my high and decided I had better forego any further cultural bonding. After considerable "eternal friendship" nonsense, this celebrity gringo managed to take leave of his fellow revelers.

The fare the taxi driver offered me was ridiculously low, so I insisted on sitting in the back, my sock-filled-with-coins-blackjack at the ready. I nearly freaked out when he told me he was stopping "to talk to a friend." As he crossed the street to inform his partner he was bringing home "green treasures," I considered getting out and running, but figured this too would be risky. Instead I got out and slowly walked down to the nearest light and proceeded to pee against the lamppost, hoping to convince them this had been the sole reason for my exit. I leaned against the post, prepared to dash into darkness if they approached.

His friend made an audible clang of the gate and feigned returning to his hovel. My driver went to his taxi and tooted, and I waved for him to come pick me up. Considerable tooting and waving followed. He finally backed up.

With no attempt to conceal my coin-laden sock, I got in the back seat. If he stopped again, I fully intended to bash and run.

When we pulled up to my hotel, I tossed the ridiculously low fare on the front seat and made a rapid retreat. Profanities greeted the dawn.

I took several deep breaths and selected the few items I could share with my sister. I was happy when this second letter arrived a few days later. It had parts I could read to her.

Fundamentalism is flourishing in South America. Bolivians seem to have one foot in the church and the other in tradition. At these services the Indians and other "true believers" wave their arms in a frenzy approaching a trance.

One of my students—a born-again Christian—invited me to a "special" church service. None of the fervent members seemed to know little other than "we're Cristianos," so I didn't learn their denomination. My student, along with several devotees, waited for me outside. They shook my hand, anticipating a new disciple, but I escaped inside so I could be alone to take notes.

After some rousing singing came the sermon.

"Children, it is the last hour! You have heard the antichrist is coming, but I am here to tell you that he is here. Bill Gates is this antichrist! Scriptures from both the Old and New Testaments make this clear. Proverbs 11:4 states: 'Riches do not profit in the day of wrath.'"

This enlightened prophet gave other references to demonstrate the dangers Gates presents to all that is right and just. His conclusion, from Acts 26:18, admonished all to open their eyes. "We have been chosen to turn people like Bill Gates from darkness to the light! From the power of Satan to God! For such a pressing need, we must give and give generously!"

The ushers unwound nylon rope to block all passages except the one past the collection basket. Two fervent, hawkeyed American con men adapted their pious smiles to the amount of shekels each true believer dropped into this viper's pit. Their pious smiles vanished when I tossed in a worthless French coin.

My sponsor and his crew were waiting for me on the steps. They greeted me with more handshakes and "How did you enjoy the service?"

I gave an honest reply. "Most interesting!" Then I managed to refuse their invitation for coffee.

This was part of the e-mail I received back on our boat in Port Marly: Am back in Lima, and all is well. The city is stimulating since there are demonstrations against President Fujimori. A drug-dealing security head has been caught on film stealing and buying votes."

When I picked Bill up at the airport, he sounded hoarse, so I asked where he had caught a cold.

"It's not a cold," he said. "I didn't want to miss the excitement, so I got too close and was tear gassed with some extra-potent stuff."

41

United States and Australia: Home Exchanges

(Ina)

After our return from South America, I said, "Bill, I think it's time we bought suitcases with wheels."

My comment was ignored.

A few weeks later, I demonstrated how easily my new luggage rolled.

"I don't know why you got that," he said. "Suitcases are for tourists. We're travelers! We need to keep our backpacks. They can go anywhere, and there's always room to stuff in one more thing."

"Space has never been my problem. You're the only one who feels the need to carry around old passports and more books than you use."

I joined Homelink, a home exchange organization, and made arrangements to exchange our houseboat and Peugeot for accommodations and a vehicle elsewhere. Getting exchanges for our Paris houseboat was so easy. I was confident that after more than ten years of vagabonding, my days of making perilous jaunts up the

Mekong in a leaky boat or zigzagging through Saigon traffic on the back of a motorcycle were over.

"Now we'll have a base when we visit," I said, "I'll no longer need to strap a pack on my back."

Bill remained dubious. "I don't relish the idea of sleeping in the same bed in the same town every night and visiting only local attractions."

I couldn't refrain from mentioning the number of nights he'd slept in the same bed in Bali without visiting any local attractions.

I should have known my dream of normal travel wouldn't materialize. We arrived in Solano Beach, near San Diego, at 4:00 p.m. By eight the next morning, Bill had us on the road.

We were on the inside of a two-lane highway when I saw a sign on the entrance to a tunnel: "YOU ARE ENTERING MEXICO."

Our exchanger had underlined in red: "OUR INSURANCE IS NOT VALID IN MEXICO! DO NOT TAKE OUR CAR THERE!"

With adrenaline pumping, I yelled, "Stop!" Bill hit the brakes and the emergency light simultaneously. He didn't yell at me, which could only mean he had seen the sign too. Horns honked as cars behind us screeched to a halt. Those in the outside lane kept moving. We were trapped. Bill jumped out and waved. A guy behind shouted, "Idiot! Did you get your license at McDonald's?" The cacophony continued until a kind soul paused long enough for Bill to shoot across. Gravel flew after he crossed the outer lane and swung in between two semi-trucks parked on the side. Two lines of one-way traffic still prevented any escape. Nonplussed, Bill said, "No big deal. I'll check this out." He went to the Mexican truck driver parked behind us. After some discussion he came back and said, "It's OK. There's no dividing barrier on that road over there." He was pointing to the highway across a pasture bordered by scrub oaks.

Bill located a narrow opening in the thicket and went back again to ask the driver to back up a few yards because he needed to angle the car to squeeze through. As he edged in, I heard scratching sounds and closed my eyes. We bounced through the pasture, around bushes and weeds, but we made it to the edge of the highway on the other side.

Two lines of cars were headed for the border. One man saw Bill's arm waving and realized our problem. He stopped traffic so Bill could drive across to the safety of the return lane. Thank goodness Americans are helpful when driving—we hadn't found as much courtesy elsewhere.

Bill took refuge in one of the border parking lots. "What are we going to do about the black scratches on their shiny white car?" I asked.

He took off his undershirt and poured water on it. After considerable rubbing, he grinned. "Look, Ina, you can't notice a thing."

Thankfully, he was right.

As we walked over the border into Mexico, he informed me this entire episode was *my* fault.

I smiled. "For someone who has lived in the Granola State with all the other fruits, flakes, and nuts, it's little wonder you missed seeing that four-foot sign."

When we sauntered along the passageway leading from the border into the city, I stopped to look in the stands selling Mexican jumping beans, piñatas, and onyx chess sets, but I quickened my pace after Bill said, "Tijuana is one of the most gangster-ridden places in Mexico."

At the main street, he began chasing nostalgia with comments like, "There are dozens of new sex bars…Look at all these shops. They go as far as we can see…They're advertising medicine without prescriptions there!"

I commiserated. "Isn't it sad? So many changes, and it has happened so quickly—in only forty years." After more prolonged "usta-ing,"—it use to be like this—we chose a restaurant. We had just finished our margaritas before five mariachis bedecked with sombreros, serapes, and silver-beaded trousers began their serenade. As they inched closer, their wide smiles broadened. We feigned appreciation but found it a bit difficult to enjoy our chili rellenos with this local color blowing so near our napkins.

Our second house exchange was in Berkeley, where we became surrogate parents to Alison and Tom, two geriatric cats. On our brisk morning walks along the old Berkeley pier, we could recognize the ever-shifting image of Alcatraz, the Golden Gate Bridge, or the San Francisco skyline, depending on the density of the fog.

Berkeley boasts a disproportionate number of gourmet restaurants, Nobel Prize winners, and street people. We didn't take much advantage of the restaurants. Bill was too busy alternating visits between the radical students he'd met during his language exchanges at the Berkeley campus with the group of dissenters camped in front of the radio station. He didn't sleep out with the activists who blocked the streets in their effort to prevent the removal of a liberal, well-liked broadcaster. He did, however, spend several evenings with them.

Our next exchange was with a Seattle couple whose home was near the University of Washington. I listened to another dose of "usta-ing": "When I was here, the gym was there...That football stadium is new...Wow, what a library they have now!"

More enjoyable for me were our five days spent at their summer cabin with my sister and her husband near snowcapped Mount Baker.

The following year I arranged three more exchanges on the other side of The States. I was a bit leery about the first one—a French provincial mansion outside Boston. When the owners asked about our housekeeper and gardener, I suggested that since we had neither, perhaps they might like to rethink the exchange. They assured me this was no problem, as they were looking for "an experience."

Bill got a strange look from their housekeeper when he arrived with his backpack, but our tenants later reported they had indeed had an experience and asked for a return engagement.

For the next exchange, we took Amtrak from Boston to New York City to enjoy the beginning of New England's famous fall foliage. Our ten-day exchange was with a lady whose recently deceased husband had been district attorney in the Bronx. Bill, loaded down with his beloved backpack, greeted the doorman effusively. From her Eighth Avenue penthouse on the edge of the theater district, Bill watched the docking of several many-storied luxury liners. From the other side of the wraparound terrace, I could read the marquee of three theaters. We got along well with Hytone, her appropriately named calico cat.

Then a second month in Greenwich Village opened up all the funky delights of the area. Bill put up his cultural-exchange sign in Washington Square. Drug trafficking must have been rampant for a regular said, "See that van over there. Two detectives are in there monitoring a screen for pushers."

Only occasionally did I ask Bill to visit a museum. His reply was always "Sitting in Washington Square reminds me of Jean Cocteau's line—'Just sit near the bar in any Parisian brasserie, and you will see theater as good as any onstage.'" Since I could speak the language, I had no trouble filling my days in this city that crackles with excitement. I reveled in attending legitimate theater with half-price tickets. I found this far more entertaining than Bill's "fascinating" dialogues with real-life ex-boxers and failed whatevers.

At the end of this trip, we returned to Paris to confront the dilemma of where to go that winter. I suggested we try for an exchange in Oz. We had listened to our Australian neighbors extol the beauty of their country for most of the years we had lived in on Le Bienveillant. Bill wasn't interested. His reason: "They speak English!"

"But it's not the same English. Everyone knows they say g'day, not hello."

"It's close enough. I spoke too much English when we were in the States. I'd rather go to Rome."

"Rome is cold at Christmas, just like Paris. It will be summer Down Under."

I wasn't making headway, so I switched the subject to boats. "I hear Sydney has one of the most beautiful harbors in the world." Not much enthusiasm. My last hope was snakes. "Bill, are you aware Australia has more poisonous snakes than any other continent in the world?"

He agreed to go but with the proviso we stay no more than one month, and return via Bangkok.

We hadn't been in Balgowlah, a suburb of Sydney, long before I was informed I had goofed.

"I can't possibly explore Australia's ethnic mix in a month. They speak two hundred and forty languages here! This is truly the land of Oz and, except for the States, one of the friendliest places we've been."

Nothing short of my getting on the Internet to find another exchange here would pacify him.

Julie, one of the women I contacted, had a unit in Manly, the beach town extolled as being "seven miles from Sydney and a thousand miles from care." She had returned from a vacation in France and had fallen in love with Paris. When she asked how long we wanted to stay, I glibly replied, "For as long as you like," thinking two months would be the most we could hope for. When she said, "What about a year?" I was somewhat taken aback. But since Bill wanted more time with their 240 languages, I took the opportunity to give him more time. I, too, was intrigued by the country and felt that at last I had made some headway with speaking their English.

Though Bill might be hungry enough to eat the arse out of a low-flying duck, after I had a squiz at the menu, I knew well it was chook eggs I wanted to eat for brekky.

And in the arvo, when we strolled over to the beach, we saw most of the littlies wearing sandshoes and sunnies. Sometimes they just ran around starkers—though this nonattire could hardly be labeled the ant's pants.

I didn't get my knickers in a knot if the bureau predicted a shocker. No worries. It never stays crook for long. After the southerly buster, she'll be apples.

I was stoked at the idea that I could twig on to more of their lingo. After all the exposure I'd had to my mate's cultural exchanges, it would be bonza if I could end up talking like a fair dinkum Aussie.

Epilogue

(Bill)

MIDWAY INTO OUR year-long exchange, we decided Australia would be a great place to live. After we jumped through a lot of hoops, we received permission to live and buy a home there. We sold *Le Bienveillant* and moved into our own terraced apartment in Manly.

During our stay, we traveled north to learn about the Aborigine languages. To promote my language exchange, the manager of a radio station in Taree interviewed and taught me a story in his language, Biripi.

While Ina became fluent in Aussie, I hosted a monthly language group reading Shakespeare in five languages. This was great fun since with our readings, even Macbeth, became high comedy. We also enjoyed a weekly creative writing group where we read and commented on each other's work.

A friend in Manly invited us for dinner with his aborigine friend who had played his didgeridoo for Queen Elizabeth. And I got to know two others who play their *didges* along the walkway leading to the Opera House.

After almost ten years there Ina and I agreed, "It's time we went home!"

We sold our unit, made a stopover in Santa Monica for a year, and are now living in Sarasota, Florida, near several friends we taught with in Belgium.

Though I promised Ina I'd be a stay-at-home, this summer we're headed for my nephew Ron Mahoney's isolated cabin in Alaska. Ina agreed, after stipulating, "After this trip, our gypsy days are over. Period. This will be our last hurrah!"

I agreed.

I'm wondering, is she right?

About the Authors

Bill Mahoney hails from Pittsburgh, Pennsylvania. At thirteen, he began hitchhiking across the country, working odd jobs. He sailed the Atlantic as a merchant marine and then the Pacific while serving in the navy. After graduating from an adult high school in Seattle and attending the University of Washington for a year, he gained a BA at UCLA and an MA in international relations from Boston University. He taught in the Los Angeles school system for three years, then in Paris, and at Supreme Headquarters Allied Powers Europe, in Belgium. He speaks five languages and can tell a story in a dozen others.

Ina Garrison Mahoney is from Blooming Grove, Texas. She holds a BA in speech and drama from Southwestern University along with a master's from the University of Houston. After joining the Department of Defense Dependent Schools (DODDS), she taught in France and the Netherlands, and then became a librarian and media specialist in SHAPE.

40660314R00140

Made in the USA
Lexington, KY
13 April 2015